4th Fashion Doll Makeovers

Learn from the Artists

by Jim Faraone

Published by Hobby House Press
Grantsville, Maryland 21536
www.hobbyhouse.com

Hobby House Press

Dedication

To Mark Ouellette, Bruce A. Nygren, Charles L. Mo and
Michael Alexander who started it all.

Additional copies of this book may be purchased at $22.95 (plus postage and handling) from
Hobby House Press, Inc.
1 Corporate Drive, Grantsville, MD 21536
1-800-554-1447
www.hobbyhouse.com
or from your favorite bookstore or dealer.
©2001 Jim Faraone

Printed in the United States of America

ISBN: 0-87588-599-3

Table of Contents

Acknowledgements

Thank you to all the featured artists/designers for sharing their time and talents with us; my father and mother Albert and Florence Faraone for their support; Charles Faraone for his computer expertise, Kerry Anne Faraone for photographing the "How To" section; David W. Simpson for his belief in me when I first started out, Karen F. Caviale and Marlene Mura of *Barbie® Bazaar* for their support of the artists, and Vicky Lewis of *Vicky On The Net* for helping me locate some of the artists being featured.

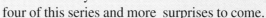

First, I would like to thank all those who have shown their support for me and my books and who have made it possible for this exciting 4th edition. Once again, I am proud and honored to feature more talented individuals from around the world and take you a step further in creating your own fashion doll wonders. For this new book, I am featuring artists, some of which create fantasy, mystical and unusual creations, for your enjoyment.

I thought it would be interesting to give you the background on fashion doll makeovers. Though extremely popular today amongst the artists and collectors, fashion doll makeovers is certainly not a new fad or craze. It actually started over 20 years ago with the fashion doll makeover pioneers Mark Ouellette, Bruce A. Nygren, Charles L. Mo and Michael Alexander (MiKelman). It was a time when collectors at first wouldn't dream of buying anything without an established manufacturer's label on it. These venturesome individuals worked hard, stood firm in what they believed, and persevered through the trials and tribulations turning what was once thought of as a "crafty" hobby into one of the most desirable "must have collectibles" in the collecting world.

Barbie® Bazaar was the first magazine to begin featuring the artists and their creations. I remember their early black and white issue featuring the first artist Bruce Nygren. Karen F. Caviale and Marlene Mura have come a long way in promoting the artists in their now wonderful full-color issues. Not only do they feature the artists and techniques in each issue, but they have also developed the *Fashion Doll MakeOver* contests each year for the international and the domestic artists. It is truly an honor to be awarded their crystal trophy and I feel that everyone who participates is a winner.

The now defunct *Miller's*™ fashion doll magazine also began featuring the artists in their issues. Barbara and Dan Miller and their

magazine are truly missed in the fashion doll world.

My series of books started out in 1996 as a black and white, self-published book titled *The Artists Behind The Fashions*. Hobby House Press was gracious enough to take it over and produce it in full color changing the title to *Barbie Doll Makeovers, Learn from the Artists*. After consideration, and not putting all of ones' eggs into one basket, the final decision was to rename the book *Fashion Doll Makeovers, Learn from the Artists*. The rest is history with book four of this series and more surprises to come.

Fashion doll makeovers have also hit the internet with many sites featuring tips and techniques on creating fashion doll makeovers. Some are excellent and some are a bit scary with uninformed individuals giving information that can ruin your dolls down the line. Please be careful when picking up tips and techniques from the net, and always check with someone who knows the true ins and outs about it all.

I have created my own free eGroups™ list on the net where artists from newbies to the professionals are welcome to join and share techniques, tips, and experiences. Various subjects are covered simply by asking a question. Some of the topics covered are restoring techniques, photographing your dolls, promoting yourself, making boxes, as well as how to create fashion doll makeovers. There is an annual swap event in which one does not have to participate. There are fashion showcases from time to time, where we show our latest creations. At times, there are

contests. At the moment, there are nearly 300 artists on the list which is well monitored in order to keep it trouble free and to teach not only fashion doll makeovers but to teach respect for one another and for one anothers' creations. If you are interested in joining this group, just email me with your name and website and I can subscribe you from my end. If you do not have a website, mail me a letter telling me about yourself, your work, and your email address.

Again, I'd like to remind you that if you are interested in possibly being featured in one of my books, just mail me some good photos of your creations so I can start a file on you. I choose the artists for my books from these files. Don't be shy, because those that know me well know I'm very down-to-earth and just one of the gang. If you are already in my files, please update your files from time to time with your latest work.

The featured artists are not affiliated with the companies that produce or manufacture the dolls on which their fashions are displayed. Though enhanced, these dolls are merely "used" as mannequins.

Feel free to contact the artists featured or myself. It's through positive communication and constructive criticism that we will grow in the future.

Jim Faraone
19109 Silcott Springs Rd.
Purcellville, VA. 20132
(540) 338-3621
Email: jimfaraone@erols.com
Website:
    http://www.erols.com/jimfaraone/

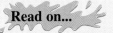 **Read on...**

Dolls are magical caricatures of people with their beauty, grace and expressive faces. Dolls remind us of a never-never land of nostalgic childhood memories, a place many of us had to leave behind as we grew up. To many collectors, dolls represent a return to the world of innocence.

This book showcases artists' interpretations of beauty and love for dolls. As you look at the hundreds of different examples and consider how you wish to design your own doll — face, hair, costume, accessories — the author and publisher would like you to do the following:

1. CAUTION - Any change to the originality of a doll can influence its resale value to a collector on the secondary market. We therefore suggest you use a much loved and played with doll in your artistic endeavor. Using these "hurt" dolls is like rescuing and preserving them for future generations. If you cannot find much loved or played with dolls, then use newly made dolls.

2. Always sign and date your work. This makes your design an original and ensures that all your hard work and dedication will be recognized.

3. Represent the sale of your work as coming from you the artist. Never represent yourself as "Jim's Barbie® doll and outfits", "Ginger's Gene® dolls", etc. Although you have created your own design for a fashion doll, that fashion doll was originally created by and the rights to the doll belong to someone else. Include a disclaimer, such as the following, in your advertising and show displays: "<u>Doll name</u> is a trademark of <u>Company name</u>. This (These) doll(s) are not sponsored by or affiliated with <u>Company name</u>."

4. Most importantly, enjoy yourself and let your creative juices flow!

Fantasy and fiction inspired me at a very young age. I remember the day that my parents caught me using their acrylics to repaint a wall in my bedroom. Frustration was obvious, but a 3-foot Mickey Mouse in Fantasia-wear seemed to fit. Since then, I have been inspired to create works of art that remind me of everything from crisp wintry mornings to rainy days to reliving a part of my wonderful childhood.

My name is Kristie Liller. I was raised in the hills of northern Beaver, Pennsylvania. My childhood was filled with adventures ranging such as camping, hiking, painting, and building. My most creative inspirations came from my parents who did not seem satisfied with life unless they were constantly creating. By watching their endeavors, I learned the passion, persistence, and patience that I hope to one day to pass on to my children.

My interest in creating BARBIE® dolls came to me in the fall of 1998 when a close friend of mine showed me his collection. He walked me through the steps that he took to create a work of art that is not so much what the item was, but rather what he wanted it to be. I immediately became hooked and started creating for myself. In the

Morning Glory

Wizard Of Oz

following weeks, I totally ruined several dolls in the attempt to recreate a look that I had in my mind. Finally, I was able to create my first work—a Raggedy Ann® doll made from a BARBIE® doll that I gave as a gift to my husband. Since that first creation, I have transformed many BARBIE® dolls into works that have not only inspired me to do others, but also revealed my true love—the creation of Tiny Treasures.

Tiny Treasures is my way of saying "No, I won't grow up, and you can't make me." Well, enough about me, onto my Treasures. Before I go, I would like to say thanks to the following people for their patience and inspiration: Christopher Clark (my Prince), LeeAnn Clark (who wants to make dolls too), my parents Harold and Stephany Liller, my sister Dawn Strealy (who maintains my website), Michael Pisocki, and the Kelly Klub.

Photos by Randy Thompson

Nuvak

Glispa

Kristie Liller
16904 Larkspur Ln., Apt. 5
Independence, MO. 64055
Email: ChrisandKris@mindspring.com
Website:
http://www.geocities.com/tiny_treasures_creations/

Scott Shore

Hello, my name is Scott Shore and I'm originally from Philadelphia, Pennsylvania. I graduated from the Philadelphia College of Art, with a degree in interior design. Before getting my degree, I spent 8 years in Lancaster County, managing three sewing factories for my family. I also designed clothing to be sewn in our factories and sold in our factory outlet. After graduating from college, I worked for some of the top interior designers in Philadelphia, PA, Washington, D.C., and New York City. I started my own design studio in 1980, working from my home in Philadelphia. I eventually moved to Florida where I worked for a large design firm as senior designer. On occasion, some of my clients (knowing my fashion background) asked me to design clothing, mostly formal gowns. I guess that is when I decided to start concentrating on fashion over interiors.

About one year ago, my partner had to have a kidney transplant. This was done in Tampa, FL. and during our extended stay in Tampa, we started collecting Bob Mackie BARBIE® dolls. I was fascinated to say the least. I also knew that I could make gowns for the BARBIE® doll and that I would try to come close to Mackie's style. Today, I have a website devoted entirely to fashion makeover BARBIE® dolls. I joined Jim Faraone's doll web ring, and have been going on from there. I have learned a lot from the people in the ring. They are all so helpful and if I ever have a question on how to do something that someone else has done, or that I have seen, I can always ask the group. I always get a few different answers. Also, I am always searching through fashion magazines and books for ideas.

I usually start with a design in mind. Then I look for fabric to complete my design. I always do a sketch of the gowns before I actually start cutting and sewing the fabric. My first step is to remove the doll's head so

Alexis

Lemon Chiffon

Tawnie

that I can root the eyelashes. Then I repaint the face and set it aside while I pin and sew the gowns onto the doll's body. I find it much easier to work without the hair in the way. To date, I have never used a pattern. I do all the work by cutting and pinning. Then I machine sew the long stretches of fabric and finish the detail work by hand. I am always on the lookout for BARBIE® doll-size jewelry and accessories. When I can't find exactly what I am looking for, I hand make it. Going to art school since I was 8 years old really comes in handy.

The manager of the local Rag Shop and Michael's® arts and crafts store know me by name and call me if they get something that they think I would be interested in. When people see me buying ½ yard (0.46m) of fabrics and feather boas, they always ask what I'm doing with them. (You can't make much with ½ yard (0.46m) of fabric). When I tell them that I do fashion doll makeover dolls, they get very interested. In fact, I have been asked a number of times to make custom dolls for people that I have talked to.

Scott Shore
2102 SW Gailwood St.
Port Saint Lucie, Fl. 34987-2202
Email: slshore@adelphia.net
Website:
http://www.geocities.com/sl_shore/

Andreas Vogel

Bagpipers Dance

My love for the little fashion doll began during my childhood in the early 70's, when I saw her for the first time. For some years, my greatest birthday wish was to have a BARBIE® doll with long hair, but that dream never came true because I was a boy. So, I played lovingly with my cousins' dolls. Over the years, the passion I had for the BARBIE® doll began fading into oblivion until the day I found the special offer "Rock Stars" Dee-Dee® doll. The passion started again, and this was the beginning of my collecting career.

I was looking for a non-blond or special-faced doll by Mattel®. I was lucky as they produced the charming Mackie mold and the dolls of the nostalgic vinyl collection. Inspired by my job as a hair stylist, I rerooted, cut and styled the BARBIE® doll's hair. But this still wasn't enough!

I began sewing for her since the day I found sewing patterns for 11½in (32cm) dolls, but the clothes didn't fit very well. So, I began to design and sew the outfits myself (learning by doing). My interests in fashion grew with the BARBIE® doll. I really like the 60's style because it was so innovative—the space look of Cardin or the futuristic style of Courrèges for example. I love to do these little leather handbags, jewelry, hats, gloves, and pantyhose and I love to remodel shoes. Sometimes I do little platforms. It's a great challenge for me to scale these miniatures because I'm a little bit of a perfectionist.

My other project focus is on contemporary fashion. The provocative Vivien Westwood, Alexander McQueen and Thierry Mugler inspire me. My creation *Bagpipers Dance* and *Fashion Gallop* are reductions of Westwood's lovely outfits. Her platform shoes are sheer genius. I tried to remodel the BARBIE® doll shoes and it was a success. With both dolls, I began with the shoes and worked to the top.

Fashion Gallop

The beginning of each doll is different and depends on the idea in my mind. Peggy Moffit was an innovative model in the 60's. Her metal evening gown in the style of Paco Rabanne was revolutionary. My *Grace of the Moonlight* wears a tight transparent organza over reflecting sequins. She sneaks out at night to catch a ray of the moonlight. *Beauty of the Jungle* was designed for the Paris Fashion Doll Festival 2000. The theme of the competition was Haute Couture. She won 2nd place from the public and 1st place from the judges. The outfit is a mixture of 1900 and 2000 and is inspired by Versace. Because I like the 20's, I composed the *Flapping Charm* BARBIE® doll. Here, I started with the little hat. I thought about how they do it normal size and I molded it in felt. Then I found the fake fur and so on. *Flapping Charm* is one of my special designs.

In 1999, with fortune on my side, I won five prizes for my makeover creations and I'm happy to get this honor. After these presentations, some people fell in love with my dolls and they asked me to sell them. First, I hesitated, but now I do! I plan to announce my dolls on the internet.

Peggy Moffitt in Paco Rabanne

Andreas Vogel
New Look
Oderstr. 20
D-10247 Berlin,
Germany
Email: new.look@t-online.de
Website: http://www.newlook-dolls.de

Morito Anjiki

My love of dolls and design began when I was a small child. Being deaf, I was always following my mother around so I wouldn't miss any bit of information that might be going around. While I was shadowing my mother, she couldn't get any of her work done. She then came up with the idea of sitting me down with one of my sister's dolls, as my baby-sitter; well it worked.

The cherry blossoms were just starting to unfold when I went with my family to visit my cousins who lived nearby. As my cousin pulled back the shoji, we entered the house. The house was filled with a kind of festive feeling. The girls in the family were setting up their display of dolls for our traditional celebration of "girls day". I was examining the display of dolls and was fascinated with the beautiful traditional kimono they were wearing. I asked my cousin where I could buy a kimono like these for my collection. She replied that I could not buy them because her older sister had made them for her. I then turned to my mother and asked if she could make me one of these beautiful kimonos, but she replied that she was too busy to make one for me.

The cherries were glistening like marbles in the warm afternoon sun when I decided to go toy shopping with money I tucked away for just this occasion. When I walked in, I spotted her lined up on the top shelf—the American Girl BARBIE® doll. The design on the box showed a beautiful doll that I had never seen before. I climbed up, brought her down, and opened the box. To my surprise, she did not look the same as the beautiful drawing on the box. Disappointed, I left her on the shelf. Later that year while visiting a classmate, I noticed she had a new doll. I told her I liked her new doll and inquired who she was and where she had gotten her. My classmate explained to me that her name was Francie® and that she was the BARBIE® doll's cousin. I liked the Francie® doll very much, but was curious why she had not purchased a BARBIE® doll. She told me that she was also a bit disappointed in the look of the doll. Later I learned that the BARBIE® doll was not as popular in Japan at that time. A few months had passed and I still had my savings burning a hole in my pocket, so I went off on another trip to the toy store. I was scanning the shelves that now contained the new boy action figures, not dolls! Standing in a new see-through box was that girl again, the BARBIE® doll. This time there was no surprise, she was displayed in full view, and she was beautiful. She was the new T.N.T. BARBIE® doll. I plucked her off the shelf and went up to the cashier. I knew then—I was hooked on the BARBIE® doll.

With their branches laden with snow, the cherry trees looked like lace woven along the countryside. I soon grew older and my studies took the place of my interest in doll collecting. Then at the age of 32, I packed up my bags and flew off to see America, a country that I had only known from my studies. Shortly after arriving in Southern California, I entered a special school to learn American Sign Language. Every country has its own sign language, and if I was hoping to stay here, I knew I needed to learn the language. The class was for people from other countries to learn American Sign Language. Our teacher, Sandra Dickinson, was very encouraging, and I met a lot of new friends. In my free time, I enjoyed sightseeing and browsing the many shops in the area. One afternoon while I was window-shopping, standing in the window of an antique shop was my old friend the BARBIE® doll, just like the one I had as a child. That outing did it again. It sparked my interest in doll collecting and there was no stopping me now.

I searched all of the stores and collected all of the books and magazines I could find on our girl the BARBIE® doll. I collected many BARBIE® dolls after that, and was pleased with my choices, but there was something missing. In the back of my mind, I could still see those beautiful kimono that my cousin had so lovingly made for her sister.

It was a hot dry summer with not a cherry tree in sight, when I decided I had time between studies and would try my hand at designing a kimono for my favorite model, the BARBIE® doll. I scoured the shops in Los Angeles' Little Tokyo for books on the subject of Kimono design. After several attempts, I became skilled and quite knowledgeable on the subject. I also had to search, sometimes for months, for just the right fabric and pattern to fit the BARBIE® doll's stature. I wanted to use silk, and with the many layers of fabric that goes into making a real kimono, this took some time and engineering. In my research, I became very interested in vintage kimono. Wanting to stay true to the period, I began dismantling an antique kimono to help fill my quest for authenticity. In this quest for perfection, I even went as far as cutting up my mother and grandmother's kimono. There are bits and pieces of my family's heirlooms all over the country on dolls I have already sold. I sure hope my mother never reads this article.

I am a frequent visitor to the Japanese bookshop in Little Tokyo. One day while browsing the bookstalls, I noticed a man, Caucasian, carrying a stack of books to the check out stand. If this were a regular bookstore I might not have noticed him, but all

of the books here are written in Japanese. I saw him arrange the stack on the counter and leave for a moment. Curious, I stepped over to see what titles he had picked up. I was amazed to find that all of his books were on Japanese dolls. I then checked to see if there were any in the stack that I had not seen. While thumbing through a book, the man returned. I think he said something to me, but I could not hear him. I tried to apologize to him and he left the store with his purchases.

That week I had heard about a BARBIE® doll show hosted by Barbara Peterson. The show was scheduled for the weekend, so decided to attend. While examining all of the tables, piled high with BARBIE® doll merchandise, I looked up to see that same gentleman I had seen just days before in the bookstore in Little Tokyo. He had his own booth and was selling dolls from Japan. I quickly went over, and on a piece of paper, introduced myself. He wrote that his name was David Hammon and that he was very interested in Japanese dolls. I wrote back that I design kimonos for my BARBIE® dolls and he expressed interest in seeing them.

After showing him my creations, he told me about a new line of dolls that might show off my designs better. It was a larger scale doll called the Gene® doll. I soon got to work designing kimonos for her, and David was right—the kimono looked even more beautiful on this new size doll. David then informed me of an upcoming convention for the Gene® doll, in Hollywood, at the old Hollywood Roosevelt Hotel. He said my designs were outstanding and that I should share my talent with others. I then got busy sewing and shopping and researching and shopping and sewing. I was exhausted.

Then came the day of the show. With interpreter in hand, we loaded up the car and were off to Hollywood. Fred Hunsberger, my interpreter, also helped me design my display. People flocked around us to see the unusual display of dolls we had created. We were a success and I sold quite a few dolls at that show. That was just the beginning. Since then, I have been to every Gene® doll convention that has come up. I even traveled to Paris to attend the fashion doll show with my interpreter and some friends.

I also have a popular webpage at www.morito.com that my friend Bob Bechtold, a great website designer, has helped me create. I hope to continue creating my kimonos as long as people enjoy them and as long as I am able. Like the cherry tree that fades into fall, it is renewed by the warmth of spring and offers us its bounty. You too should use your creativity to its full potential and share your bounty with others. So, get those creative minds blossoming and those sewing machines running. If a deaf man from Japan can do it, so can you.

Morito Anjiki
471 S. Fairview St.
Burbank, CA. 91505-4713
Email: loveo@morito.com
Website: www.morito.com

Janeece

Hi. My name is Debbie Hendrickson, designer of "Something Different Creations". My love for dolls started with my Skipper® dolls when I was young. They had an extensive wardrobe made with love by my mother. However, once I hit my teens, I thought I was too old for them, and gave them away to some younger girls. What a mistake that was! I regret it to this day! I didn't get back into dolls until after my three kids were born, and I began to play dolls with them.

My husband had his hobbies, and the kids had theirs. I wanted one too. When I saw the first Little Debbie BARBIE® doll advertised on the back of the snack boxes, I knew what I wanted. My husband encouraged me to get the doll, and that was the beginning of my collection. Immediately, I had to have more dolls. In the middle of moving from one side of the country to the other, I was buying BARBIE® dolls like a crazy woman.

Once settled into our new home, I found a *Barbie® Bazaar* magazine in the bookstore and was thrilled. A whole magazine just for dolls! With that, I found that more dolls were available than just what department stores carried, so I began to amass the more elaborate collectable dolls. My favorite articles in the magazine were on the different doll artists, and the creations that they made—such diversity, such imagination in their dolls. Not the usual fashion or play dolls, these had truly one-of-a-kind personalities. Then my husband did something drastic. He told me that I needed to learn to use a computer in order to get on the internet. I balked, but he sought out different doll lists and sites for me. This encouraged me to talk with others online. I was no longer the only person who collected dolls. There were many of us, and some of those collectors were doing amazing work with their dolls!

Empress Monarch

It started as one little doll swap, an exchange of customized dolls, and I was hooked. There was no limit to what a doll could become—from a Leprechaun to an outer space beauty, to a butterfly, or even to look as though she were made of stone! Thus, "Something Different Creations" was born. My philosophy has always been "uniquely customized" so you will not find "just another pretty doll in another pretty dress." Dolls must have their own personalities. Very rarely will I make more than 2 or 3 of any single doll, and even of those, they are not exactly the same. Repetition becomes monotonous, so they must all be new and different.

All my dolls are founded in fantasy, whether they are mythical or historical. I strive not so much for accuracy, but for the whole image that the character brings to mind. Until now, most of my dolls have been fairly simple in design, without a lot of fuss and frill. I am trying to create designs that are more elaborate by using beadwork and trim. My only complaint with this is that it takes so long, and time is something I am severely lacking most days. If I am rushed on a project, I won't be happy with it, and if I am not happy with it, then it just isn't good enough. So, things have to wait at times. I am truly looking forward to the day when I can stay home and work on my dolls all day long, rather than go off to work while the dollies wait at home, half-clothed, half-scalped, half-painted.

I do want to express my thanks to everyone. To my husband and kids for allowing me to play dolls instead of cooking dinner. To all my internet friends who encouraged me as well and filled my head with compliments on my dolls giving me the courage to list my dolls on the internet where they have been appreciated as well. To Dorothy, who forced me to send my pictures to Jim, and to Jim, for all the work that goes into putting this book together. Finally, thanks to God for giving me the imagination and creativity to enjoy this task.

Lady Arachnia

The Fountain

Debbie Hendrickson
Something Different Creations
626 Mourning Dove
Newport, N.C. 28570
Email: jhendrickson@coastalnet.com
Website:
http://www2.coastalnet.com/~b8w8z6mh/mom.htm

Cynthia Luna

Sunsprite

My first BARBIE® doll was the very "first" BARBIE® doll. In 1959, I was shopping with my mother as the store was setting up the display of BARBIE® dolls. There she was—the perfect doll! I couldn't believe it when my mother bought me one right then and there! I guess she could see it in my eyes. I was in love!

I have always loved dolls, though I didn't have many as a child. I learned how to sew for myself by sewing clothes for my BARBIE® doll. When I was in high school, that BARBIE® doll went into the closet and only came out from time to time with the excuse of making clothes for the little girls in the neighborhood. I was a closet BARBIE® doll fan.

I have been involved with dolls in one way or another all my life. My grandmother had a fascination with dolls, and I think that I inherited that trait. At one point, I made reproduction clothes for antique dolls. I have made and collected many different dolls in my life, but I always come back to the BARBIE® doll.

I have enjoyed entering the world of fashion doll makeovers more than I can say, and I learn more and more all the time. I have met many wonderful and talented people in this fascinating world of doll makeovers and I'm proud to be in this book amongst some of the best!

Angelique

Cynthia Luna
14834 Hartsville St.
La Puente, CA. 91744
Email: luna@tstonramp.com
Website:
http://www.barrysdolls.com/bellaluna/index.htm

Tribal Dancer

Anita Healy

Dolls have always been a big part of my life. I started collecting at a very young age and continue to do so. My customizing began about a year-and-a-half ago when I went online in search of a doll discussion group. I finally came across one and shortly after joining, was introduced to the world of fashion doll makeovers. To date, I have created and sold well over 100 dolls.

The dolls I create can be best described as runway inspired made of high quality fabrics, fully lined clothing, realistic repaints, elegant hairstyles, and special attention paid to detailing. My husband Jimmy creates each box by airbrushing the display boxes to match the doll's theme.

Photos by Jimmy Healy

Winter's Beauty

Anita Healy
A Brooklyn Doll Shoppe
1650 E. 7th St.
Brooklyn, N.Y. 11230
Email: AHealy9011@aol.com
Website:
http://abklyndollshoppe.homepage.com

Ella Trumpfeller

Val de Grace

My passion for collecting fashion dolls began in 1996. Within a few months of connecting with other collectors on the internet, I became the co-president of the US Chapter of Dolls International Prestige Collectors Club founded in Italy. This club has over 50 members internationally.

My customizing of fashion dolls began in 1998 by sheer accident. I decided to trade my childhood vintage Francie® doll to one of my club members, so I carefully wrapped her in pretty tissue paper and shipped her off. I had no idea what a mistake I had made. The pretty tissue paper had ink in it that absorbed into the doll's body in various locations. Upon learning my mistake, I got the doll back. Because she had a spot on her nose that was obviously not removable, I decided she would make a cute cat.

I'd never re-designed a doll before and I didn't want to start with my Francie® doll, so I borrowed a couple of my husband's 12in (31cm) comic hero dolls (X-men's® Storm® and Rogue®) and transformed them into cats. To my surprise, upon posting pictures of them on the internet, they quickly sold and numerous

Emerald Fantasy

Peek-A-Boo Kitty

potential buyers contacted me for more dolls. Eventually, I did makeover my Francie® doll and sold her as well.

I did not even know there was a makeover community at that time. My love for cats originates from "Cats" my favorite Broadway production, which has always had a special appeal because of my own dance background. I have been the owner/director/teacher of the "Dance Centre School of Dance" and "Body Design Dancewear" (retail store) since 1982.

My first cat makeovers sported ears of mesh-covered wire and whiskers made from doll eyelashes super-glued to the face. I've now matured to sculpted ears and rooted whiskers. From 4in (10cm) miniature dolls to 15in (38cm) dolls, I've created a variety of characters. I've made cats and kittens, fairies, mermaids, drag queens, trailer trash, and specialty dioramas. Cats, however, remain my specialty. I've learned to root eyelashes, re-paint faces, and many other customizing skills through my Egroup™ connections with other fashion doll makeover artists. I makeover 50-75 dolls per year.

I have donated dolls to conventions, charity events, and have participated in swaps. My greatest joy now, in addition to dance, is working with my dolls in addition to communicating and helping others on the internet with similar passions. I welcome others' makeover ideas and freely share my own techniques as well. The makeover industry has grown so much in the past few years and I'm very happy to be a part of it.

Ella Trumpfeller
2151 Harvey Mitchell Pkwy So.
Suite 105
College Station, TX. 77840
Email: Ella@purrfashiondesigns.com
Website:
http://www.PurrFashionDesigns.com

Kevin Allen

I have loved dolls for as long as I can remember. When I was young, my cousin Susan and I would spend hours playing with her BARBIE® dolls. No one really thought it was strange for a boy playing with dolls, because I grew up in the middle of nowhere. I had no children to play with, except Susan. As I grew older, I lost my interest in dolls.

My interest returned about four years ago after seeing the great lines of collectible dolls on the market. I started collecting the BARBIE® doll. By this time, I had internet access, so a whole world of dolls was opened to me. I joined a mailing list about the BARBIE® doll. There I found some doll artists and when I saw their work, I was amazed! Needless to say, I had to try fashion doll makeovers myself. I learned some of the various techniques— painting, rerooting, and things like that. I soon became frustrated because I would make a doll that would look good and then I would be forced to put her in a store bought fashion. That wasn't good enough for me, but I just didn't have the sewing skills that I felt necessary to be a true doll artist. So I put it aside and just continued with doll creating. But, the bug had bitten me!

In December of 1999, I told my mom Margaret that she had to teach me how to sew. She promised me she would, but with

the holidays, we never got around to it. On Super Bowl Sunday 2000, I went to her house, we pulled out the sewing machine along with some fabric and a basic pattern and I began. I never realized how much was involved with sewing until she started teaching me. "A dart isn't something you throw at a board?" She definitely had her work cut out for her, but she succeeded. I left that day with a doll in a simple dress, and boy was I proud! Since then, I have been learning new techniques, asking a lot of questions, and making a lot of friends.

Since becoming a doll artist, I have found a way to sneak back into my childhood, to recapture my youth, and to PLAY again! The nice thing is, STILL, no one thinks it's strange!

Kevin Allen
936 Shive Ln. #167
Bowling Green, KY 42103
Email: mimmit@msn.com
Website:
http://members.fortunecity.com/kevinnbg/originals.html

Terri Norcia

My adventure as a doll artist began when I first encountered a repainted Gene® doll on an online auction in March of 1999. At the same time, Ashton-Drake introduced the new Simply Gene® doll. I was excited about the prospect of doing makeovers on this doll and immediately bought several Gene® dolls to repaint and restyle. Having nearly 20 years experience as a licensed cosmetologist and make up artist I left the field due to allergies and because I had a desire to help people. I went back to college to become a counselor. I never realized how much I missed the creative aspects of my life until I became absorbed and obsessed with repainting dolls. I found it difficult to tear myself away to do anything else. At the same time, I had a compelling desire to learn how to do a website so I could share my pictures. I love photographing my dolls just as much as I love creating them.

Wanting to find others with a similar passion, I learned about Jim Faraone's Fashion Doll Makeover discussion group online. I wanted to share my pictures of my dolls to get objective opinions and to learn what I could do to improve them. I remember praying as I sent my pictures to the list that no one would hurt my feelings. I was immediately flooded with emails for three days for requests to repaint collectors' dolls and so many questions on how to repaint. There are no words to express my total shock and amazement to the reactions and compliments. This all occurred the same week that I was informed that my agency where I do counseling was losing its funding and due to major changes in my profession, my unhappiness continued to grow. At first, I turned down all the requests, but as I learned how much more bleak things were going to become in my profession, I decided that I would at

least take a step in faith and repaint just a few dolls for people. I marveled that someone would be willing to pay me for doing something I absolutely loved. The requests to do dolls grew and grew fast. For eight months, I was customizing four dolls a week for people at a pace I knew I could no longer keep. I felt uncomfortable about increasing the prices, but it was the only way to decrease the number of requests. Presently, I have only been offering dolls on an online auction and no longer take commissioned dolls.

In the past, I have dabbled in painting with oils and sketching faces, but did not have any experience with acrylics. As a therapist, I worked a great deal with survivors of abuse utilizing art therapy. My family and teachers always encouraged me to pursue an interest and training in art, but I never believed I was good enough. Instead, I went into the beauty field because I had a passion for doing makeovers on people and loved the result of helping them feel better and more confident about their appearance. The most difficult part of repainting doll faces was learning how to master and control this type of medium. My passion keeps me dedicated and determined to

continue until I get the face that I'm hoping to achieve. None of my dolls ever live up to what I imagine, but I love the challenge and the opportunity to improve on my last doll. I rarely do anything the same and have no secrets. My advice when asked how to repaint is study faces and practice, practice, practice!

The reward in doing makeovers is not only the pleasure I receive in creating a new face and feeling a sense of accomplishment, but also the positive responses from the people who write me. It used to take hours of counseling sessions to help people feel better. I now find it quite fascinating and ironic to read how the faces of my dolls bring people an immediate sense of peace and happiness.

Terri Norcia
3338 Leonard Ave. SW
Canton, OH. 44706
Email: galaxyofglamour@aol.com
Website: http://www.terrinorcia.com

Sandy Cunningham

Tory Trudeau

Awake in a dream world of glorious fabrics, lush furs, sequins, beads, glitter, delicate trims, ruffles, lace, paints in a rainbow of hues, all stand ready. Vinyl doll bodies of all sizes abound. Oh my! Some of the dolls have no heads! But wait! Across the room are the missing heads, adorned with lovely technicolor hair. A sewing machine and a monster magnifying light stand center stage in this riot of color. You have just experienced a mini dream tour through the workroom of "Fantasy Design" and "Fantasy's Tiny Folks".

Hi! I am Sandy Cunningham - aka - San C. mistress of this wild, crazy and wonderful realm. I have been collecting fashion dolls for about six years. In the beginning, I was an avid NRFB collector of everything from pink boxes to the top of the line expensive Mackies. After several years, the boxes take over your house and you have to go in a different direction—the deboxer was born. About this same time on vacation to my favorite city, Las Vegas, I fell in love with the costumes of the showgirls. Very easily lured by my love of glitter, glitz, and fantasy, I thought, why can't some of my dolls be showgirls? Once home, the quest began to gather supplies to make my first showgirl. What fun she was to create! Dressed totally in red feathers, fringe, and red jewels, I called her *Ravishing Ruby*. Ruby now resides in the collection of a customer in Texas. Many showgirls have followed in Ruby's dancing shoes, and my dolls are at home in collections throughout the US. Around the same time I finished my first doll, I acquired Jim Faraone's wonderful books about doll artists and design. I was forever hooked into the world of fashion doll makeovers.

I have taught myself to paint faces, dye and style hair, root lashes, and costume dolls. No, you don't have to have a fancy diploma from a big school of fashion design to try your hand at doll artistry. Another helpful tool to new artists is the internet doll artists and collector groups. I have learned so much from Jim Faraone's Fashion Doll Makeover artist group. Most of the artists there are like family—all helping each other with tips, ideas, and most of all, support for one another. Branching off into the world of the "lil' folks" at the Kelly® doll Klub net site, I have found a new group of friends and artists in a whole new medium—tiny 4in (10cm) Kelly® dolls. It's a fun challenge. I prefer the Candi® doll and Alyssa® doll for showgirl makeover dolls because they look so grown up and exotic. Fairies are my second love and I have created some high fashion dolls as well.

I have to credit treasured friends and other artists who have helped and encouraged me in my artistic endeavors. My "doll buds" Gwyn, Paula, and Donna (who bought my first attempts at fashion doll makeovers) and are always my cheerleaders. Ms. Ella is my fellow artist friend and the "cyber-wizard" behind my beautiful website. Many loving and sharing doll artists who lend their expertise daily, Jim Faraone, William Stewart Jones, Dorothy Fannin, and Dan Lee. Last and of utmost importance is my wonderful hubby Ray who is a constant source of support, praise, help and a lender of fantastic creative ideas.

If you think you want to try doll designing, my advice is to go for the gusto. You only go around once in this world so try it. Doll designing (or playing dolls, as I call it) gives hours of fun and relaxation. In addition, you will meet the nicest and most talented people in the world connected to this craft and you will acquire friendships that last a lifetime. The most important factors when considering doing a fashion doll makeover is that you must have a love for dolls and a vivid imagination. Create your designs to please yourself and let your imagination run free—the sky is the limit

I am thrilled to be living out my fantasy through the dolls you see pictured with my story. My designs are featured at live doll shows throughout Middle America. They have also appeared in the showroom and auction at the National BARBIE® doll Convention at Tulsa 2000. Visit us at a doll show in your area.

Zulu Warrior and his Queen

Sandy Cunningham
2033 Deer Run Circle
Muskogee, OK. 74403
Email: barbies@azalea.net
Website:
http://www.angelfire.com/ok3/fantasydesigns/index.html
or http://sandesigns.tripod.com/tinyfantasy.html

31

Jean MaDan

Candi Kisses

My name is Jean MaDan. My husband John, my two sons, and their wives have been a cheering section for me. That makes it possible for me to do this work full time. The house has been taken over by dolls and fabrics, and it isn't unusual to find the occasional sequin floating in the bathtub. Through it all, the support has remained at high tide with no complaints! (Or at least, none they've been brave enough to share with me.)

I started doing fashion doll makeovers in 1999 when I was unable to do construction work any longer. It may seem like a long stretch to go from roofing, drywall, plumbing, electrical work, and brick laying to doing fashion dolls, but it really isn't. Construction techniques are much the same for dolls, though on a MUCH smaller scale. It's still a matter of attention to detail, form, and function with a strong eye towards beauty. And I don't have to worry about falling off the roof!

Loving dolls the way I do, and having learned to sew when I was only 5 years old, it seemed so natural for me to switch to fashion doll makeovers. I saw my first fashion doll makeover on eBay in June of

Blue Waltz

Cherries Jubilee

1999, and thought WOW! I want to DO that! So, I grabbed up a well-loved BARBIE® doll purchased at a yard sale, and began learning! Like a lot of things that I've attempted in my life, it turned out to be more difficult than it looked! (Oh my! That poor BARBIE® doll!) Of course, in hindsight, I realize now that I did just about EVERYTHING wrong. Being too stubborn to give up, I marched myself to the bookstore and picked up some new "how-to" books. It really seemed strange not to be picking those books up in the hardware store! After learning the techniques I needed to do successful doll makeovers, I was able to concentrate more on polish and developing my own style. I've branched off to include the Gene® dolls, which I really love working with, as well as some of the other dolls like the Elle® doll.

I'm still learning new things daily in this field, and it's such a joy to work with something that yields so well to personal taste and definition. I plan to be doing this for as long as I can hold a brush and see the paint! I'm constantly amazed and impressed by the beautiful work other artists are doing in this field. The only drawback I've been able to find so far is that my wonderful husband and sons can no longer do the Christmas shopping for me at the home improvement store, but hey, that's THEIR problem, right?

Photos by Jim Batchelder

Jean MaDan
41886 N. Coyote Rd.
Queen Creek, AZ. 85242
Email: MADAN49@aol.com
Website: www.madandolls.com

Kelly Hannon

A DINK ("double income no kids"), I am a legal secretary for a labor law firm in Atlanta. My husband Larry and I share our house with three spoiled rotten Himalayan cats. My sister and I had the Madame Alexander® 8in (20cm) and 10in (25cm) dolls as children. In late 1998, I discovered eBay and the ability to return to my childhood by acquiring dolls like I had as a child. Thus, I became an eBay junkie. I also discovered that prices for the vintage dolls were more than I was willing to pay, so I decided simply to make copies of the rare outfits. I learned that I needed hats to go with so many of the outfits, so I took on that challenge. When I counted 14 barefoot Cissette® dolls, I realized that I needed to learn to make specialized Cissette® doll high-heeled sandals, too.

Larry and I are avid, if not good, golfers. I am also a computer addict. I thoroughly enjoy my email buddies whom I "met" through eBay (Hi, Kathy, Thea, Ann, Ronna, Susan, Melinda, Becky, Paula, Peggy and Patricia).

Creations of costumes worn by Vivien Leigh from *Gone with the Wind*.

Creations of Gail Davis in *Annie Oakley*; A Safari outfit; Blue velvet riding habit.

Titanic; Renoir; Julie Andrews in *Throughly Modern Millie*.

Kelly Hannon
628 Washington Dr.
Jonesboro, GA. 30238
Email: khannon@constangy.com
Website:
www.photopoint.com - View Friend's Albums - enter
email, kellyh@constangy.com

Joan Champagne

Although I was always surrounded with dolls as a child, my passion for doll collecting surfaced within the last two years. When I was growing up, I took dance, piano and voice lessons and was always in the school plays and eventually the various theater groups in our town. After I graduated from high school, I moved to New York City to attend drama school. Like most struggling actors, I had a variety of jobs to support myself. I did everything from temporary office work to teaching ballroom dancing at one of the major studios in NYC. Being young and impatient, I didn't stay in drama school long. Instead, I got my first job in a summer stock company. After that, I continued doing dinner theater work, summer and winter stock, off-Broadway shows, and many road shows.

I love New York and the theater people I met there and though I eventually left the City, I never lost contact with some of the dear friends I had made there. In fact, one of those friends introduced me to the world of doll collecting. She had also left the City and moved to Pittsburgh. She had also developed an interest in collecting dolls. If you are a doll collector, you know that it doesn't take long to get "hooked" and she was. We used to talk on the phone once in a while and a lot of the conversation related to her doll collecting—what she was going to buy or what she had already acquired. Well, I got the point and when she was hospitalized for major surgery, I bought her a doll and got the same one for myself. Shortly after that, I was at an auction and won a 1993 mint, never removed from box, Holiday BARBIE® doll. I got it for fifty dollars and was thrilled though I didn't know its actual value. Soon, I was buying almost every BARBIE® doll I saw—pink box, collector—it didn't matter. I am interested in all kinds of dolls though my preferences are mainly fashion dolls.

Broadway Baby

In 1998, I got my first computer and discovered the Internet. There I found people who actually created fashion doll makeovers by re-rooting, re-painting, and making wonderful, original clothing. I decided to try it myself and then created a website to display my creations.

I have been doing fashion doll makeovers for over one year now and I never stop learning thanks to all the talented artists who are so generous in sharing their experiences and knowledge. I have created various types of dolls but I am starting to focus on my favorite styles, which are day and eveningwear from the 1940's and 1950's. I am an American Movie Classics TV fan and I get many of my ideas from watching the old movies. I also enjoy creating dolls that represent places that I have been or that I frequently visit.

Doing fashion doll makeovers is a new experience for me and I am just beginning. I have found a new creative outlet and I am really enjoying myself!

Joan Champagne
18 Nelson St.
Glens Falls, N.Y. 12801
Email: Showdolls@goplay.com
Website:
http://www.angelfire.com/biz3/ny2/index.html

Debi Jacovelli

Wisteria Fairy

I have found that being a fashion doll artist requires me to be part-artist, part-seamstress, part-computer programmer and webmaster, part-graphics artist, part-photographer, and part-jewelry crafter. And I have to admit that at times I find it all quite challenging! It all started simply from my love of both the BARBIE® doll and butterflies. Let me explain.

When I look back on the path my life has taken, I can see how all the pieces have fallen into place. First, there was my father who was an electronics technician. He taught me how to solder a skill I use now when creating rhinestone necklaces and he was instrumental in encouraging me in the arts and music. He was a very creative individual who did the layout of his own newspaper ads for his business. Then there was my mother who draws very well. I have early memories of the two of us sitting together with a piece of paper as she showed me how to sketch a face. I enjoyed art throughout my school years and was often chosen to make covers for school booklets and play programs. I won several awards for my drawings. I went on to study art in college and later taught classes in watercolor and clay to adults and children.

My love for fashion dolls began as a young girl when I received the first brunette ponytail BARBIE® doll. She was joined by a blond bubble-cut BARBIE® doll and then by a flocked-hair Ken® doll. My doll collection continued to grow, as did my love for them. Growing up with three brothers, my dolls were my female playmates. At the same time,

my grandmother was working at the original Burlington Coat Factory® in Burlington, New Jersey. She took the time to teach me to sew using her old Singer® treadle machine. I learned the art of hand-sewing using scraps of leftover fabric that my grandmother would bring home from work. She even made a full-length fur coat with a matching hat and muff for my beloved BARBIE® dolls. Thanks to my grandmother, my dolls had the best hand-made clothes in the neighborhood! Even today, when frequenting yard sales and flea markets, I find that the doll outfits I treasure most are the ones that are handcrafted!

I continued sewing for myself as I got older. I even designed and made my own wedding dress, my mother's gown, and my husband's white tuxedo. I became a tailor, and made custom clothes and did alterations for a few years. In addition, I spent some time making soft sculpture dolls and selling them in consignment and craft stores.

The BARBIE® doll became a part of my life again in the early 1980's, after I had long since given away or lost my original dolls. To my delight, my husband came home one day with a gift for me—a Malibu BARBIE® doll and Ken® doll! After a few years, I started collecting new fashion dolls and rescuing them when found at thrift shops and yard sales. Currently, there are over 500 BARBIE® dolls and other fashion dolls in my collection.

Living in South Florida with its warm climate all year round has enabled me to

Forest Flower

pursue my other hobby—raising butterflies. Over the years, I've developed an extensive butterfly garden in my backyard. Though it requires a lot of time and careful attention, my hobby has allowed me to enjoy the pleasure of nurturing and propagating about 30 different species of butterflies. If you've ever spent time in a butterfly garden surrounded by the beauty of countless butterflies in flight, you can understand how such an environment fills one's mind with thoughts of whimsy. Hence, the fashion doll artist was born.

It occurred to me one day, "What would the BARBIE® doll look like with butterfly wings?" I thought that with all the dolls I had that I'd give it a try to see if I could transform the BARBIE® doll into a work of fantasy. I created one of my first dolls with wings crafted from iridescent fabric, fabric paint, glitter and glue. One thing led to another, and I found a wonderful sense of pleasure in creating the fashion and fantasy dolls you see pictured on these pages.

To do a fashion doll makeover, I remove all the face paint and repaint it, adding lashes and other features. I then redesign the hairstyle (sometimes re-rooting the hair) and create a unique outfit and jewelry for the doll. I then make the doll available on my website or, at times, on Ebay® auction website. Maintaining my website has given me the opportunity to develop my skills as a computer graphic artist. Developing all the images and graphics to keep my website up-to-date proves to be as enjoyable as creating the dolls themselves.

Above all, the greatest joy for me comes from knowing that a doll which starts as a simple sketch on a piece of paper ultimately becomes a work of art possessed by of one of my dear customers who loves her as much as I do. It gives me pleasure to know so many different people enjoy my work. This is the very best reward that any artist could ever have!

Pink Chiffon

Debi Iacovelli
Golden Girl Designs
Email: debi@goldengirldesigns.com
Website: www.goldengirldesigns.com

Joanna Bond

Web Creature #32324

I grew up in a creative household, surrounded by songs, murals, and stories. I believed that our hilly Pennsylvania acreage was home to fantastic beings. As life knocked me around a bit, I channeled my fantasies into writing, collage-decoupage, and kitsch, like gluing objects that I found to furniture. I also started collecting toys never losing my taste for make-believe.

Fashion dolls became a medium when I kept finding myself bringing home well-loved dolls like stray cats. They were always tattered and lonely, used-up by their previous owners! One day, I picked up a half-bald doll and decided to fix her up. I learned how to re-root her hair from a well-timed *Barbie® Bazaar* article. A few hours later, my fingers were bleeding, but the doll's smile was brighter, and I was hooked.

I didn't just want to restore dolls though. I found myself looking at my other toys and thinking things like, "Wouldn't it be cool to have one with pink hair?" or, "If Mattel™ doesn't make a centaur BARBIE® doll, I will." These thoughts were fleeting at first, as I still had to get my feet wet. I started with existing characters like She-ra®, Wonder Woman® and Xena® just trying to make versions that you couldn't buy in stores. Eventually my other instincts emerged, and I began transforming dolls outside of the proverbial box. My old techniques of decoupage and glue took over. I've even been known to write stories to accompany my dolls. I'm not sure exactly where my ideas originate, but they're always there.

I prowl thrift stores and flea markets for interesting dolls to rescue, and craft stores are paradise. I love to break the rules of what constitutes doll hair, clothing,

Esme Centaur

The Goddess of Treasure

or wings. I like the shock of metal wings, for example, or iridescent plastic hair. Irony, spirituality, music, and the human mind inspire me. Conceptual warriors and mythical creatures pepper my universe. A fashion doll is not a mannequin, but a canvas.

As serious as I sometimes have to be as an adult, toys remind me that a playful imagination is a powerful gift. Like my mother, I encourage my kids to sing, paint, and invent, and we do a lot of that together. I love allowing creativity to flow.

Joanna Bond
7911 15th Ave. SW
Seattle, WA. 98106
Email: mojo@freakydeakydolls.com
Website:
http://www.freakydeakydolls.com

Chandra

When I was in high school, my art teacher told me that I had no artistic talent and that I should quit wasting my time. Well, that set me off on a quest to prove him wrong. I taught myself how to make miniature teddy bears, as well as develop my own patterns. I then taught myself how to do miniature porcelain dolls. I entered one of my first dolls in a local doll show and won first place. I was so thrilled because I had taught myself and competed against very experienced doll makers. Well, that was the beginning of my fascination with doll making. Then I saw the BARBIE® doll makeovers in Jim Faraone's book. That is all it took. I sold my kiln, not because I thought I would ever sell a makeover, but because of my total fascination with the makeovers (and because my electric bill was getting a little too high.)

My specialty is fantasy because I love it so much. The BARBIE® doll's little sister, the Kelly® doll, has really caught my attention lately and provides a challenge that I love. In working with her, I have stepped out of normal fantasy characters into mod, glamorous, and even comic book characters. I still do the BARBIE® dolls and the Kelly® dolls in fantasy. I love to make them up as fairies, mermaids, and centaurs. My dolls have been accepted in many markets. I have sold them and traded them to people all over the United States. Thanks to the internet, I have placed my dolls around the world from the Arctic circle to near the Equator.

I would like to thank my husband and daughter for having to eat so many Hamburger Helper® meals so that I could complete a doll that was just begging to be finished. My goal in doing fashion doll makeovers is the same as my goal in life, to simply bring a smile to someone's face.

Shelly Norrick

Renaissance Angel

Magpie and Chestnut

Shelly Norrick
Norrihollow Custom Creations
3946 SW Haverhill Rd.
Lot 27
El Dorado, KS. 67042
Email: mnorrick@aol.com
Website:
http://www.crosswinds.net/~norrihollow/

Angie Gill

It all started when I was a little girl. If it wasn't "BARBIE® doll-sized," then I didn't want much to do with it! I come from a family of four girls. I got all the good hand-me-down BARBIE® dolls from my older sisters, and boy don't I wish I still had them. We lost all of our BARBIE® dolls when we were little and moved from Ohio to West Virginia. Who would have guessed that my design work would stem from that loss? In 1998, at the age of 28, I was missing those little childhood girlfriends that my sisters and I had, so I set out on a mission to replace them. I started to browse for them and discovered the ghastly cost of mint vintage and mod-era dolls. So, I decided to buy them in poor shape and restore them. I started sharing my work with others. I picked up a few regular customers, and then the next thing I know, I am on eBay seeing all these lovely one-of-a-kinds that different artists made. A whole new world opened to me!

I have a wonderful mom who taught me everything that I use to create my dolls' costumes. She sews with the most professional care and attention to detail that I have ever seen. She was a stay at home mom, and is still very crafty. Everything I learned, I learned from my mom as far as my doll crafting abilities go.

If someone were to ask me for advice on making dolls, I would tell them these things. First, stay away from original work. Make sure your designs are just that—YOURS, not someone else's. Second, take your time and use only the highest quality supplies you can find because a short cut will eventually show in your work. High quality does not always mean that you have to pay the highest price for them either. Keep your eyes out for sales and ALWAYS look in the remnant bins at fabric shops!

I start my makeover by styling a doll's hair. Then I paint the face, create the outfit, and make her jewelry.

The last thing I do before putting her jewelry on is to root her lashes. I do that last so that they do not get pushed in while handling her as I bead her outfit.

I love making my Gilly Gals, and although the birth of our first baby has slowed me down a bit, I hope to always be able to sneak some time into each day to do my "dolling"! I have to give a lot of thanks to my husband, Rob. He has always supported me and was the one who taught me how to master my website. He is the one that I turn to for advice regarding Gilly Gals! I don't think that I would be making dolls if it weren't for his loving words of encouragement.

Angie Gill
Gilly Gals
3027 Addison Dr.
Grove City, OH. 43123
Email: Angie-Gill@GillyGals.com
Website: www.GillyGals.com

Viktoria La Paz

Some of the most famous artists throughout history are known for their predilection (or obsession!) in painting the feminine face in a certain style. We need only gaze upon one of these painted faces to recognize the artist who created it. The idea to re-style a fashion doll to match the image of feminine beauty held in my own imagination was a temptation I could not resist! Therefore, my desire to create a recognizable face of my own as well as my wish to incorporate the same art media that I use in my illustrative work inspired the concept of "Illustrated Girl" fashion doll re-paints.

As an internationally exhibited fine artist and illustrator, I work primarily in colored pencil. I wanted my dolls to possess the same soft texture and blended appearance of pencil art. My technique creates the same elements that make up a colored pencil by layering graphite or charcoal, opaque inks, beeswax, and resin resulting in a doll of realistic tonal shading and textures. A combination of storybook fantasy and realism brings an ethereal gracefulness to a doll's face while retaining a life-like demeanor.

While any doll I meet may fall under the attentions of my busy brushes, my current energies are concentrated on some of the popular 15in (38cm) and 18in (46cm) fashion dolls. These include Mel Odem's Gene® doll, Robert Tonner's Tyler® doll, Esme® doll, and Kitty Collier® doll, Madame Alexander's Alex® doll, and Effanbee's Brenda Starr® doll. My re-paints are available through direct sales, auction, and at times, by limited commissions. For inclusion on my Doll Alert Mail list and for more information, visit my website.

Viktoria La Paz
Illustrated Girl Fashion Doll Re-Paints
P.O. Box 230772
Tigard, OR. 97281-0772
Email: illustratedgirl@crazyredmare.com
Website:
http://www.crazyredmare.com/illustratedgirl.htm

Tangren Alexander

Egyptian Ambassador

Marketplace Children

I'm a philosophy professor at Southern Oregon University, and I still play with dolls and, in a way, believe in them. I don't make over dolls in order to sell them, but to rather to create characters and scenes for people in my 11½in (29cm) world. I like to use a variety of races, ages, and body types. I also love well-jointed dolls that can move more naturally. If I could ask for one thing from Mattel™, it would be jointed wrists like the Living BARBIE® dolls had. When I modify my dolls, I try to bring out their human qualities. For modern-day characters, I often take the makeup off, make eyes smaller, cut hair, and work on eyebrows. Other times, the characters are fine with the faces they came with, but they get new hairdos and costumes. I've also made furniture, rooms, and sets for my dolls.

I often photograph scenes that I've created. I've developed slide shows of my photographs that "combine cultural criticism with the sweet magic of belief" to make stories in which the dolls come alive and have adventures giving them deep and meaningful lives. My largest work to date, a slide show on which I've worked for over 20 years, is an enactment of a children's book by Z. Budapest, *Selene, The Greatest Bull Leaper on Earth*. It's a story of a little girl raised in ancient Greece who returns to her mother's home in Crete. With hard work, courage, and the help of the Goddess, she learns to overcome fear and become a bull jumper. It stars a particularly soulful and well-jointed Living Skipper® doll sold as the Swing-A-Rounder Skipper® doll in the seventies. It also features the Malibu BARBIE® doll, Grandmother Heart® doll and Growing-Up Skipper® doll in supporting roles.

Flower-Bearing Celebrant

Keeper of the Labyrinth

Snake Priestess

The pictures shown here are all "extras" in a scene set in the marketplace in Crete. I've cut and sometimes curled the hair of the little kids. The older children wear dolphin armbands made from ear cuffs. One holds an octopus toy that her grandmother made. The adult figures are from a scene of a sacred procession that winds through the marketplace. The Posh Spice doll plays an Egyptian ambassador and Benjamin Franklin puts in a cameo appearance as a flower-bearing celebrant. The Teresa® doll and Kira® dolls act as a snake priestess and a keeper of the labyrinth. All these dolls came with makeup that was already perfect for their parts. For some, I created new hairstyles. My assistant, Mariah Hegarty and I made costumes based on our research into ancient Cretan styles for all the characters. There are many more where these came from.

My work has been mostly shown at academic conferences. I'd love to present it at a BARBIE® doll convention sometime.

Tangren Alexander
200 Ashland Loop Rd.
Ashland, OR. 97520
Email: tangrena@internetcds.com
Creations by Tangren Alexander

Curtis Hammond

I grew up in a dusty little town on the eastern plains of Montana, and in my earliest daydreams, I wanted to be an artist. In Montana, the true artists were Russell and Paxson, and their art captured the people and rough landscape of the West. Because my ability (and desire) to draw cowboys on horseback was limited, I found respite among the funny pages. I drew inspiration from Snoopy® and Pogo®'s escapades, and I especially loved Blondie® in her fashionable tailored suits and dresses. I drew hundreds of paper dolls, and by doing so, learned to appreciate line and form.

My first fashion doll was a discounted Marie Osmond® doll, all hair and teeth, grinning boldly in her outrageous purple gown from the top shelf at the drug store. She was on sale for $0.99 and I bought a birthday card too in case the clerk grilled me as to why a thirteen-year old boy would purchase a doll. I figured that I would quickly explain that it was a gift for my sister. My heart raced as I placed the doll and the birthday card on the counter. I couldn't wait to get Marie home and make her a thousand new outfits from my mom's bin of fabric scarps. It was the beginning of a sweet addiction.

After Marie, I bought a leggy Mego™ Wonder Woman® doll which led to a Superstar BARBIE® doll. When I bought a Kenner™ Bionic Woman® doll, I decided her body was entirely too masculine. My efforts to clothe her in elegant evening gowns made her look as though she were a weight-lifting drag queen. The purchases continued with a succession of other dolls. My collection of tiny dresses, suits, coats, and gowns were all hand-sewn (Mom guarded her Singer™ closely) and numbered over 500 by the time I was 16. Each outfit was titled and logged into a special secret notebook.

Among my creations were "Cotton Candy", a poofy tiered cocktail dress of enormous bubble gum pink polka dots and "Olde Velvet", a Victorian style walking gown cut from a weighted dark green velour making it the most elegant jogging suit the BARBIE® doll ever wore. With the other 498, I spent many happy hours of my youth designing, cutting, and sewing. I shared some of them with my niece, Becky, and we dressed and redressed the girls, dreaming up fantastic tableaus with them prominently featuring their impressive closet.

I stopped designing for fashion dolls by my late teens, but I couldn't stop sewing. By then, mom thought me trustworthy enough to use her sewing machine, and I was busy building costumes, sewing quilts and creating cloth dolls. After some 15 years, fashion dolls have again charmed me. I have Jim Faraone's first book to thank for restoring my interest. I began making and selling angel dolls with faces sculpted from Fimo®. One day, while browsing the doll section of a local bookstore, hoping to find some inspiring cloth doll books, I came across Jim's first book. I admit that I haughtily thought to myself, "These aren't REAL artists, like me! I'm making the entire doll—they're just painting a BARBIE® doll and putting her in tight

clothes!" Then I paused to recall what it had been like to design and sew for dolls. I recalled how it was to snap a new ensemble to her frame for the first time and see how she looked. I remembered that happy time in my life when I let myself create and enjoy without restriction. I bought the book and soon found myself wandering the aisle of pink boxes at the local 'Mart re-acquainting myself with her majesty with the perky smile and eager blue eyes. Before long, I had boxes of naked BARBIE® dolls, Kira® dolls, Ken® dolls, and Midge® dolls, most of them flea market treasures sent to me from a friend in Seattle. Now there is no turning back. I have fully immersed myself in that play-scale world, acquiring stockpiles of fabrics in every shade of the rainbow, a cupboard full of laces; tins of tiny buttons and glass beads; and bins of sequins, feathers, and ribbons. My sewing room shelves are lined with cigar boxes marked "Jewelry Fixin's", "Cool Trinkets", and yes, "Bald Heads" (I'm not a very prolific re-rooter).

My dolls and ensembles have been well received by the community of collectors as well, and I have been extremely fortunate to have sold pieces to people worldwide. It's a joy to hear from folks who feel like it is Christmas when a package with one of my creations arrives on their doorstep. It makes me proud to think that something from my heart, that I've spent time making, is a treasured piece in their collection. I'm very grateful to each and every one of them for purchasing from me.

Looking to the future, I know fashion dolls will be part of my artistic endeavors. This rewarding pastime has brought me new friends and has allowed me to embrace that little boy inside of me gazing up at that grinning Marie Osmond® doll—and I don't have to buy anymore birthday cards!

Photos by Terry Cyr

Curtis Hammond
1735 B Park Place
Missoula, MT. 59802-1773
Email: chammond@qwest.net
Website:
http://www.users.qwest.net/~chammond

Linda Payne-Sylvester

I guess my first recollection of sewing was when I was about five or six. My mom had shown me how to go "in and out" with a big dull needle and embroidery thread. I remember practicing on my dad's handkerchief, which I snatched from his bureau, but as I recall, he wasn't too thrilled about it. My first doll fashion was a caftan-shaped dress which I wanted my mom to sew for me on her sewing machine. Because she probably had a lot of other things to do, she declined, but my persistence paid off because she decided to show me how to sew on the sewing machine. She probably realized that as a fledgling designer I'd be bugging her all the time with sewing requests! She taught me how to sew and she still offers lots of sewing tips today.

Like many other kids, I became enamored with the BARBIE® doll for which I designed lots of outfits. I began to think about being a fashion designer when I grew up. My best friend and I spent our time together by dumping cartons of fabric scraps out onto the floor and sewing for our dolls. Because both our moms sewed, there was never any shortage of fabric. My industrious grandmother, who turned out a staggering number of quilts, braided rugs, and fancy doilies for a steady clientele, unknowingly nurtured my love of color and design. Waking up in the morning under a heap of her colorful quilts provided plenty of visual stimulation. And of course, watching a steady diet of old movies on TV with actresses wearing stunning costumes had more than a little impact on me. I thought Loretta Young's entrance was the absolute ultimate glamour.

My career choice vacillated between fashion, painting, and graphic designing while I was in high school. After leaving home, I attended the Boston School of the Museum of Fine Arts where I studied painting and printmaking. Printmaking became my passion, and since I had to work my way through school, I usually had part time jobs in small printing and publishing companies. I also became interested in photography which, along with my printing and publishing experience evolved into a career for over twenty years. During much of this time, studying ballet kept me in touch with the art world where I encountered opportunities to either sew or design costumes for small theater, opera, or dance productions.

A few years ago, my last job became more and more computer centered, and although I loved learning technology and creating digital photo imagery, I was feeling the desire to express my creativity in more tactile ways. My love of and appreciation for crafts and fashion design began to resurface. After seeing an infomercial on TV about BARBIE® doll collecting, my husband, feeling that I needed a fun hobby to balance the pressures of the workplace, suggested that I start collecting dolls. I began collecting just as the Gene® doll came along. Of course, after I had collected several Gene® dolls, it was natural for me to want to photograph her. That led to getting permission from

Night and Day

Galaxy Girl

Web of Desire

Mel Odem to photograph and market a line of Gene® doll greeting cards under my graphic design business Reflected Light Design. But I was hesitant about sewing for her because it had been so long since I had sewn anything so small. My mom, who by this time had been doing doll restoration professionally for a number of years, kept encouraging me to try it and so I did. I was pleased with the first few outfits I made and gradually gained the confidence to design and make accessories for the outfits.

Usually the fabric is what inspires me. I like working with both new and vintage fabrics, but vintage fabrics instantly inspire a design. I don't refer to a photo or anything specific. I just let the visual fashion memories of an era float around in thought while I drape the fabric on my model. Sometimes I can see the design all at once, but other times the outfit will evolve in stages.

I'm really enjoying the fact that a dream that I had as a kid is finally being fulfilled in such a fun way. Designing for dolls is very satisfying because it brings together such a wide array of creative skills. I've also enjoyed meeting and making friends with other doll collectors and have appreciated all their encouragement.

Linda Payne-Sylvester
63 Pine Hill Rd.
Cape Neddick, ME 03902
Email: lindapaynesylvester@hotmail.com
Website: www.reflectedlightdesigns.com

Osvaldo Vazquez

My name is Osvaldo Vazquez and I am the creator of the designs that you are looking at here. I was born in San Juan, Puerto Rico, but I have been living in New York for the past 20 years. I work for a major tour operator in New York City and my hobby is in the designing field. Living in New York, the "fashion capitol of the world" widens my imagination of what I want to design. One of my favorite designers is Bob Mackie. Maybe that's why I love to work with so many crystals and sequins. I have only been designing for two years, but I am very proud of what I have accomplished. One of my creations was on the cover of a fashion doll magazine and was a third-prize winner in *Barbie® Bazaar* magazine in the bridal category. I am also pleased with how my dolls are selling on eBay, but when Jim Faraone notified me that I would be one of the artists featured in his new book, it blew my mind away. For me, that's the most prestigious honor as a fashion doll makeover artist. I will always thank him for giving me the opportunity to show my creations in his book.

When I start designing my creations, I have two things that I want to accomplish. First, I want to design a dress that looks real. Second, I want to create the most glamorous girl there is. Here is the result of those two goals. I hope you enjoy looking at the dolls as much as I enjoy making them.

Osvaldo Vazquez
3111 Heath Ave. #56-B
Bronx, N.Y. 10463
Email: Ovaz340178@aol.com
Website: www.ovazdesign.com

Michelle Lester

Making over fashion dolls is really a joy for me. To take an ordinary doll and make it into a unique individual gives me such a sense of accomplishment. I just love watching each doll's special personality emerge. Sometimes it's quite difficult to let one go to a new home leaving me with just scraps of material and a photo.

I grew up with a mother who is extremely creative and artistically gifted. I remember some of the incredible outfits and gowns that she made for my dolls when I was young. I spent many years watching her work, developing a love for fine materials and the ability to spend many tedious hours working on a small piece of something.

Because I grew up in a military family, I moved all over the country as well as overseas. I was always making, coloring, or painting something from girl scout crafts to projects that my mother gave me. It filled the time between losing old friends and trying to make new ones. I also spent a huge amount of time reading. I love fantasy, sci-fi, and horror books, and many of my dolls reflect this love.

Lycan

My first "big" project was a stuffed teddy bear. My mother didn't think I would be able to do the bear alone, so I set out to prove her wrong. I'm stubborn and I didn't come out of the sewing room until that bear was finished. I still have it in my bedroom. From there, I began designing one-of-a-kind bears and stuffed dolls to sell to the military ladies and at craft shows in Germany. When we moved back to the States, I took a class at a local college on making fancy dresses for little girls. The class taught me how to make my own dress patterns and how to combine different elements to create a completely unique dress. This fueled my interest in designing pageant wear when I had a daughter of my own. I took what I had learned from watching my mother and from the dresses I made and created stunning one-of-a-kind pageant outfits for her to wear. Others soon wanted my creations and I spent several years making dresses and costumes for children's pageants, winning many awards for those designs. When my best one-of-a-kind doll decided she didn't want to compete anymore, I turned to fashion dolls. My housemate, Robin, had always loved music, so I made a one-of-a-kind Bret Michael (Poison) doll for her. I used a "Beast" doll since he had long blond hair. I did a partial repaint and made a cool rock outfit for him. I didn't know how to do eyelashes or re-root the hair at that point. Next, I made a Lady Death doll after my favorite comic book character. I

Bret Michaels

Whist

built up her breasts and rear to match the over-done female comic lady's proportions. Robin remembers laughing at me for days on end as I blew gently on the BARBIE® doll's backside, trying to get the porcelain compound that I used to set. I still didn't know how to re-root hair, so I improvised by spray painting her hair white. Later I did a complete re-root which I liked much better! I kept making dolls, and through the internet and Jim Faraone's first book, I learned how to re-root hair, root eye-lashes, and get all that pesky original paint off of the doll's face. Robin finally talked me into selling a doll, and with her support and urging, I finally did. I don't think I would have ever sold one if she hadn't encouraged me and kept telling me my dolls were good enough to share with the world. I try to give each doll a very special look, and I am usually surprised by the direction it takes. I just go with the flow, changing things as I needed in order to suit the personality that is emerging. I search jewelry stores, thrift stores, and through my own stuff to find the perfect jewelry and accessories. I want the whole vision to be complete. I deco-rate the stand that holds the doll so that it does-n't detract from the doll. I sew everything that

can possibly be sewn. I reserve glue for tiny rhinestones and jewels that can't be sewn on. I think that every fashion doll out there has a special look just hiding inside waiting for a makeover artist to uncover. Some scream out to be a fairy and some just have to be a mer-maid. Others want that special evening gown and incredible updo. As a makeover artist, I am responsible for making each doll all he or she can be. I want each new owner to enjoy my work for years to come, to find themselves stopping whatever they were doing just to look at my creation and be happy that they own it. I am thankful for my mother's gift of creativity and for Robin's never-ending support and patience. Without the two of them, this would never have been possible.

Michelle Lester
These Dreams by MichL
100 N. Briarwood #121
Yukon, OK. 73099-2215
Email: keyimason@hotmail.com or keyi@mmcable.com
Website:
http://www.geocities.com/Heartland/Pond2808/thesedreams.htm

Diane Kolodziejski

I was a young teenager when the first Cissy® doll was introduced in 1955. I still have that doll as well as 150 others! The wonder of opening a box and seeing her is still a special memory. Like all Madame Alexander™ dolls, she was beautifully dressed, but something inside my young soul wanted to put new and different clothes on her. A lifetime of sewing and designing began at that moment. Sewing for the Cissy® doll was abandoned around the time I started high school. I became more interested in sewing clothes for me, and made virtually all my clothes from that time forward. For a time, I was so obsessed with sewing that I made many dresses I never even wore. When I was a young married woman and an even newer at-home mother, I began sewing for friends in order to earn extra money. Making doll clothes had been put on the back burner for

Art Deco

many years until my daughter got her first BARBIE® doll. I still remember remodeling a Christian Dior gown for a client and then using the left over fabric to create a one-of-a-kind, beautifully beaded BARBIE® doll bridal gown.

After a divorce, a very successful career, and an early retirement, I was blessed with granddaughter, Olivia. When she was about a year old, her mommy asked me to make clothes for Olivia's baby dolls. This fit well with the heirloom sewing I was doing at the time. I bought several little girl-type dolls and made heirloom dresses for them. Then I remembered the Cissy® doll. She later turned up in my ex-husband's attic, and since she had been kept in her original box, she was in good shape. It was a tearful reunion.

I bought several Madame Alexander™ 21in (53cm) portrait dolls and one of the new Cissy® dolls, the Tea Rose Cissy® doll. I started sewing period costumes for them. When it came time to work with the Tea Rose Cissy® doll, I discovered that she had a wonderful figure much like the BARBIE® doll. So, I made evening dresses and afternoon dresses for her. All the while, my collection of dolls to use as models was growing. As any Cissy® doll collector can tell you, these dolls (perhaps because they are larger) are quite clever and know how to use the computer to order more companions and even bid on eBay.

Several of my friends suggested that I start a business selling the Cissy® doll clothes.

Medieval Queen

A Day at the Races

I laughed, wondering who would pay that kind of money for doll clothes. Eventually, I did several shows and the dresses did sell. Because of their size, it is hard to take everything to shows and you never know how many Cissy® doll collectors will be there. So, after the second show, I decided to do a website featuring clothes for the Cissy® doll. "Small Wonders" was born. It took a while draping the doll to copy Erté designs from the 1910's and 1920's. I also recreated many of the Vionnet designs. Her creative use of the bias and draping are amazing. I use lots of embroidery in my designs. I now scour the catalogs for the latest fashions.

Some of the best things about sewing for the Cissy® doll are that she never gains an ounce, she holds still for hours while you are draping on her, she never complains, and she doesn't need a special place to wear the fashions. All of this opened up a whole new world for me. I can now create all the dresses that I always wanted to make and I don't need a place to wear them. Of course, they always look marvelous on the Cissy® doll's lovely figure. Many times fabrics and even trims are the inspiration for the designs. Some fabrics just speak to me. Embroidery designs inspire me as well. I can picture, for instance, a lovely flower embroidered on her dress and embellished with rhinestones or beading. I

believe my fabric collection grows almost as fast as my Cissy® doll collection. I feel the Cissy® dolls are so lovely that I choose not to repaint them. However, I frequently change their wigs.

Recently, I discovered how much fun hats are. I have doll-sized hat blocks so that I can shape hats of real straw, felted furs, and velours. I like to block a group of hats and then sit on the floor with my trimming all around to decorate them. It makes quite a mess, but it really gets my creative juices flowing.

I am sure I will be doing this forever, because I have so many ideas in my head that I will never be able to make them all. Besides, it will take at least two lifetimes to use all the materials in my "stash". I am extremely honored to be included in this book. I hope you enjoy looking at my dolls as much as I enjoyed making them.

Diane Kolodziejski
Small Wonders
4050 Via Dolce, #342
Marina del Rey, CA. 90292-5256
Email: dkolo@mediaone.net
Website: http://www.cissyfashions.com/

59

Dan Lee

Hi! My name is Dan Lee and I'm the man behind "Wide Eyed Girls" (the name is taken from a song by the Eurythmics, my favorite pop group). I'm twenty-seven years old, single, and living in San Francisco though I was born and raised in England. From a very early age, I was a doll lover and the BARBIE® doll has always held a special place in my heart. I fondly remember sneaking into my sister's room to play with her dolls, abandoning my Action Man® figure for a life filled with glitter and glamour. My first BARBIE® doll as an adult collector was the Glinda® doll from *The Wizard of Oz* almost four years ago. From that point, my collection has snowballed—the BARBIE® doll is now my drug of choice! During the last year, my interest shifted to the TNT's and their MOD outfits.

It was eighteen months ago that I was first introduced to the wonderful world of making over my favorite piece of vinyl. My dear friend and fellow customizer in England, Suzanne Boteler, made a Las Vegas showgirl as a Christmas present for me. She also gave me a book on the BARBIE® doll that pictured other artist dolls. I was intrigued. Upon returning to the States, I went surfing on the internet and found sites with instructions on re-rooting and re-painting. Together with some basic sewing knowledge garnered

from my Granny Dunford along with trips to fabric, craft, and bead stores, I began creating my own makeover. About six months later, I discovered the Egroups on the internet for doll artists where I was able to pick up tips and tricks from others. That elevated my work to a whole new level resulting in the dolls seen before you.

My favorite part of the process is the re-root, which I do with every doll to give them fantasy hair colors. I find it relaxing, and I enjoy the feeling of creating from a completely blank canvas. Each outfit is entirely hand-sewn, as are all sequins and beading. Crystals are secured by prong settings. In the last few months I have also begun creating my own shoes using RTV molds and resin as my girls were screaming out to me for funkier, ankle-breaking shoes. Because I work full-time and have a busy social life, each doll takes roughly a month to complete. I try to fit some customizing into each day as it's now one of my great passions—nay—obsessions in my life. I'm always looking forward to getting off work so that I can get home and create as it helps me wind down from all the stresses I encounter with my job. Inspiration for my dolls comes from everywhere, but especially from 60's MOD, 70's disco, and today's nightclub scene. I think I live a vicarious life as a drag queen through my dolls.

I'd finally like to thank all my friends and family (you know who you are) as well as the Goddess within and without for all their love, support, encouragement, and patience. I couldn't have done it without all of you.

Dan Lee
1139 Market St., #149
San Francisco, CA. 94103
Email: WideEyedGirls@hotmail.com
Website:
http://community.webtv.net/WideEyedGirls/WideEyedGirls

Michael Scott

I grew up in a small town in Alabama, and fashion dolls fascinated me from an early age. I was especially fond of the BARBIE® doll. I enjoyed playing with her clothes and experimenting with her hairstyles for hours at a time. My mother bought a sewing machine when I was 10, and I ended up spending more time on it than she did. I taught myself to sew and eventually made clothes for my mother and myself.

As I grew older, the dolls took a back seat to other interests, but I was always intrigued by fashion, hairstyles, and the glamour of old movies. After earning an accounting diploma from a local junior college, I decided that I wanted to be a cosmetologist instead. In 1986, I met my best friend and business partner, Cindy Wilson Stumpe. After working together for 14 years, we now own our own salon.

My passion for dolls returned in the mid-1980's, and I became a serious BARBIE® doll collector. I thought that no other doll could compare to her until I met the Gene Marshall® doll. She and Mel Odem have really changed my life. There is no comparison between getting a new doll that has to stay in a box in order to remain collectible and a doll that can be taken out of the box, played with, and even restyled that still maintains her value. I have had more fun with the Gene® doll that I could have ever imagined. I started experimenting with the Gene® doll's hair shortly after I bought her, and it wasn't long before I started to sew for her. I experimented for several months, and after much encouragement from my family and friends, I decided to try to sell some of my designs. They did very well, and Phillip, my partner, set up a website for me. I was in business! I now sell my designs directly through my website, and I am getting ready to attend my second Gene® doll convention.

Sewing is very therapeutic for me. It has always been a way to help me relieve stress. After a day at my

job, which can be very hectic and noisy, it is so relaxing to come home, sit down at my sewing machine, and let my mind focus on what I am making. When I am not at work, I can usually be found at my sewing machine. I guess you can say that I am obsessed!

I try to experiment with all types of designs, but my absolute favorite is the elaborate gowns from the 1940's and 1950's. I don't shy away from using as much fabric as I can either. I have always admired Christian Dior. He is one of my favorite designers. A wonderful aspect about the Gene® doll is that she looks great in just about anything, whether it is a tailored suit or an elaborate gown.

My design technique is probably unconventional as compared to most designers. First, I have no drawing talent whatsoever. In fact, I can't draw a straight line with a ruler. I see designs in my mind or I will wake up in the middle of the night with an idea that I will hastily sketch on a pad that I keep by my bedside. The next morning, I usually look at what I drew only to find a puzzle that I must now put back together. More often, I simply sit down with my material and play with it until an idea comes to me. My main inspiration typically comes from the fabric itself. When I see a piece of fabric that is suitable (not always easy because scale is most important), I first think of what hair color it will accentuate. Once I get started, everything usually falls into place, and I get more inspiration along the way for accessories such as hats, capes, and jewelry. My designs sometimes turn out to be completely different from what I first had in mind.

Restyling the Gene® doll's hair has proven to be more difficult than the BARBIE® doll's hair. You would think that since I am a

professional cosmetologist that it would be a breeze, but that has not been the case. It usually takes me several hours to achieve the look I want. I usually relax the hair with hot water so that I can start with it completely straight. Then I begin cutting and thinning the hair keeping in mind that this hair will not grow back! The thinning process is determined by the style. I might only thin the back or thin it all over. I always make sure that the scalp doesn't show. This gives the style a natural look and keeps it in proportion to the doll. The last part of the process is curling the hair whether it is a simple flip or a classic bob.

The bob's are harder to create than anything else. It is sometimes difficult to reduce the bulk and keep the simple tapered lines.

My favorite aspect of having this part-time business is when I hear from someone who has just received one of my designs. They seem so happy and are so kind to compliment my work. This gives me so much encouragement to begin my next piece. I just know that one day I will wake up with no more ideas. Then I'll just look at a piece of fabric—that will keep me going. I really get excited over fabric and what it will grow up to be.

I would like to take the time to thank Jim Faraone for inviting me to be a part of his book, and Phillip Oliver for maintaining my website and photographing my work. Thanks to all the fellow Gene® doll fans that I have met through the internet and at the conventions, and last but not least, to all my clients who keep me going.

Michael Scott
Michael Scott Designs
502 S. Cedar St.
Florence, AL. 35630
Email: michael@michaelscottdesigns.com
Website: www.michaelscottdesigns.com

Photos by Phillip Oliver

Trish Walker

After years of suppressing my artistic talents with a boring career in finance, I managed to escape the ball and chain for several years of college and branched off into computer technology. This brought me a little closer to my creative side and opened some doors of opportunity. While working on my web page design, I discovered BARBIE® dolls on the internet. My collection started with a couple of retired dolls, one being my prize possession, Empress Bride, signed by my favorite designer, Bob Mackie. I admire his style and use of sequins, which I later carried into my own designs.

Shortly after beginning my collection, I became interested in the vintage BARBIE® doll and the challenge of obtaining rare fashions and accessories from the 60's. This is when I noticed a shortage of vintage jewelry, so I started designing replicas for collectors to complete their outfits. The pink pearl set was my biggest challenge since I could not find the exact size pearls in the right color pink anywhere. Needless to say, I discovered my own way of making pink pearls in order to produce the accessories to match *Fashion Luncheon*. Soon after this, Mattel™ came out with reproduction

Ocean Sapphire

Turquoise Butterfly

Amethyst Rose

BARBIE® dolls wearing fashions that included this jewelry. I knew it was time to move on to something else. During this time, I received several requests to make jewelry for the Gene® doll, so I began designing for her using beautiful Swarovski rhinestones and crystals to match her era. Making jewelry came natural to me since I've always been into arts and crafts, and I used to help my sister make beaded earrings for her jewelry business back in the 70's.

It wasn't until March 2000 that I started designing fashion doll makeovers sort of by accident. I was getting ready for the Tulsa Oklahoma show and decided I needed models to display my jewelry. This is when I designed

my first sequined mermaid *Pearl Bride*, which introduced a whole new avenue of design and a new way of life to me. As it turned out, I sold so many mermaids that I had to reorder dolls and supplies to make more for the show. Since then, I started several other series (*Beauties of the Sea*, *Sparkling Starlets*, *Jeweled Butterflies*, etc.) and have designed at least 40 OOAK fashion doll makeovers, all of which found happy homes around the world. It's an awesome feeling to do something I enjoy so much, and an inspiration to meet so many talented designers and wonderful collectors. I've always enjoyed giving gifts to others, so I design each doll as a "gift of beauty" for others to enjoy. This brings me great pleasure.

Pink Sapphire Mermaid

White Magic Fortune Teller

Amethyst Stardust

Trish Walker
Tricia's Treasures
3701 Inglewood Ave., Suite 315
Redondo Beach, CA. 90278
Email: DollBoutique@aol.com
Website:
http://www.angelfire.com/TriciasTreasures/index.html

William Stewart Jones

Queen of the Night

I didn't buy BARBIE® dolls for my daughter when she was young, so of course, now I have to buy Mackies for her! A few years ago, her boyfriend gave her a Mackie Masquerade® doll, and my daughter said, "Daddy, you can make dolls as beautiful as this. Why don't you make me one to go with my Mackie?" So I took a white blond superstar face doll (I didn't know there were other faces. I bought her for the hair color) and made her into a very overdone Marie Antoinette! She was outrageous with lots of white iridescent trims, flowers, lace ruffles and glitz! I didn't give dolls much more thought until I was recovering from major surgery and was unable to do much. My daughter brought me Jim Faraone's first makeover book. I was fascinated. I saw all the clever artist remakes of fashion dolls and I was hooked! I had never even thought of repainting a doll's face! I started designing dolls in my head because I was too weak to draw with a pencil. Soon however, I was sketching ideas in a notebook.

My first total makeover was "Tatiana", which won the 1999 BMAA Crystal Award for Fantasy. Though everyone else was doing fairies, I chose to make a doll based on a makeup I had done on my daughter for a theatrical poster. The doll's hair is hundreds of pieces of wire and the entire doll was repainted lavender. The flower

skirt is wire inserted into holes drilled into the body. Some artists are very strict about sewing everything, but many of my dolls are sculpted and constructed. My son, Nicholas, and my daughter, Kimmerie, are very encouraging and often give me good ideas for my dolls.

After many years as a Professor of Theatre Design, designing costumes for shows and private clients, and working as a makeup artist for the San Francisco Opera, it's fun to paint and costume small figures that don't talk back. I can create costumes that no stage performer would dare to wear or are too fantastic to be practical.

Because of my years as a costume designer and puppet maker, I had boxes of fabrics, feathers, jewels and trims on hand. The challenge of finding trims and fabrics in perfect scale for the small figure is a great part of the joy of fashion doll makeovers. I always sketch costume designs first. I have notebooks full of ideas. Then I usually draw an actual-size sketch to be sure of the scale of the costume elements. It's a great way to decide if a trim is overpowering or a detail is not big enough. It also helps me when I need to shop for a specific item. I make all of my patterns often working from historical garments and costume books. Just as with life-size costumes, I fit muslins onto the dolls, usually making several versions until the fit is right. I select fabrics for color, drape, and texture, and I often dye and paint fabrics and trims to get the look I want, antiquing the bright new colors and metallics to soften them. Furthermore, I usually wash fabrics so that they drape better.

My work tends to be a bit odd. I don't do standard dresses, but rather prefer the more unusual and theatrical dolls. My dolls have won awards for fantasy, history, and the outrageous! For more than 18 years, I was the costumer for "Beach Blanket Babylon" and worked with them on the 1989 Academy Awards. My costumes have been exhibited at the De Young Museum and the Detroit Museum of Art. My other work can be seen in the Academy Award winning film *In the Shadow of the Stars* and in *Tales of the City*. They have also appeared in *Time* magazine, *Life* magazine, *House Beautiful*, *House & Garden*, *Theatre Crafts*, and many, many other publications.

William Stewart Jones
152 Lily St., Apt 1
San Francisco, CA. 94102
Email: wsjones@basingstoke.org
Website: http://www.basingstoke.org/

69

Jennifer Sutherland / Annie Muscatelli / Chrissy Stewart

Demi Moore

My sister (Chrissy Stewart) and I (Jennifer Sutherland) joined as a team in the early part of the year 2000 to create dolls full of Beauty and Fantasy. Annie Muscatelli (our mother) uses her poetic ability to enhance each doll with a poem or short story. This, as a whole, creates "JaC Designs."

We begin by dreaming up a theme for our doll. After the face has been fully repainted (face repaints done by Jennifer Sutherland), we then decide what her costume will be (clothing and jewelry created by Chrissy Stewart). Each costume is wonderfully detailed to give the full effect of what we are trying to achieve and capture. After the doll has been created, the theme is then captured in a poem or short story. Each of our dolls comes with a signed and dated COA from JaC Designs, and a copy of the poem/story, if requested.

Our dolls are influenced by the romantic styles of the past, with an added touch of imagination! By combining these elements in our dolls, we hope to bring life to them.

We would like to thank Jim Faraone for these wonderful fashion doll makeover books, because we could have never achieved this without him! The best advice we can give anyone that would like to start creating is to read these books and let your imagination soar!

Xandra the Gypsy

Jennifer Sutherland/Chrissy Stewart
JaC Designs
Email: Kinnipeli@msn.com
Website:
www.geocities.com/jac_designs/index.html

Katharine Rayland

Tonner American Model® -
Gown by Marsha Olson, Jewelry by Victoria Garnier

Like so many things in my life, my discovery of the Gene® doll was sheer chance. While shopping at a local drug store in the spring of 1996, I walked by a magazine rack and saw the Blue Goddess Gene® doll on the cover of *Collecting Figures®*. Being a huge 1940's movie buff, I was completely entranced by the photo. I picked it up and went back to the counter to wait for my prescription. I secretly read the magazine and ate up every word about the Gene® doll. I had to have it! I went up to pay for it, hiding it under my arm, deathly afraid that someone would see me buying such a "frivolous" magazine. After all, I wasn't one of those silly, fanatic doll collectors...or was I?

An illustrator/graphic designer by trade, I was always fascinated by portraiture even as a child. My mother was a gifted artist and trained me right from the beginning. As a teenager, I studied under Claude Merrill, a great artist, teacher, and friend who taught me everything I now know about this artistic observation. After I received my degree in Advertising, I went on to study under airbrush master, Michael Cacy and renowned sports illustrator, Bill Vann—both of whom opened up entirely new worlds of technique and skill to my illustration work.

By the early summer of 1999, I had been at my regular nine-to-five job as an illustrator/graphic designer for many years and had amassed a collection of more than 30 Gene® dolls, costumes, and countless BARBIE® dolls. I was officially a doll fanatic. It seemed only a matter of time before the two worlds would collide. So, when someone suggested to me that I use my illustration background and apply it to fashion doll repainting, I was intrigued by the idea and decided to give it a try.

I had an Iced Coffee Gene® doll with its neck partially broken, so I chose her to be the first victim. It

Rose®

Gene® -
Jewelry by Sue Harrison

was nerve racking and exciting! It became almost madness as I eagerly repainted doll after doll in my collection, learning more with each one that I attempted! I shared the photos of my dolls on the internet Gene® doll bulletin boards. Soon, I was receiving requests for commissions and started taking in work. My very first doll taken in on commission was a Sparkling Seduction Gene® doll. That was the beginning of a long line of dolls flooding my home. I was forced to stop taking commissions in early November 1999, as I became completely overwhelmed with work and repaints. Exhausted and feeling burned-out, I was on the brink of quitting and never repainting another doll.

It was about a month later when, on a whim, I put one doll totally of my own creation on eBay to see if I could make a little extra Christmas spending money. It did phenomenally well. In March 2000, one doll that I put up for auction sold for over $1,000—a feat never achieved by any repainter selling a nude doll until that point. Such high prices are becoming more commonplace now. Dolls that have been repainted by skilled artists are being treated as the individual pieces of art that they always have been and not merely as repainted fashion dolls.

I am happy to say that I hope to continue fashion doll repainting well into my future. My work was recently featured in the *Fashion Doll Scene®*, and I will be writing a series of articles for the *Here's Looking At You* Gene Club newsletters and for *Dolls In Print®*. In addition, my dolls will be featured in a local art gallery in the spring. Fashion doll repainting is becoming more and more respected as a new art form. I feel extremely fortunate that I was there to see it happen and to help it along just a little bit.

Photos by Albert Santacroce

Katharine Rayland
Email: raylandrepaints@hotmail.com
Website: www.raylandrepaints.com

Michelle James

I'm originally from Jamaica, West Indies, but I've grown up in New Jersey since the age of 7. After attending college, where I received a degree in Computer Information Systems and Data Processing, I moved to Florida where I now reside with my husband, Charlie, and our two children, Jasmyn and Marcus.

If you had told me that by the age of 34, I would be obsessively involved in customizing BARBIE® dolls and the collecting of BARBIE® dolls, I would have thought you were off your rocker and laughed in your face. Until 1997, I had no interest whatsoever in dolls of any kind, and really only remember having one doll when I was little. I was more into books and reading, so it was no major trauma.

I've been collecting dolls since 1997 and customizing the BARBIE® doll and other fashion dolls since the summer of 1999. However, I've been crafting and creating things all my life! I've dabbled in painting, done floral arranging, decorative T-shirts, and many other types of crafts. I was led to fashion doll makeovers while surfing online one day. I came across Jenn Scully's site, and found the instructions that she had posted on how to do rooted eyelashes. That inspired me to do my very first BARBIE® doll makeover. After getting over the shock of how pretty my new doll was, I was hooked! I love doing all different styles of dolls, but my absolute favorite theme is fantasy design. I can really let my imagination soar with fantasy designs—nothing is off limits!

Some of my designs are planned weeks in advance, step by step. Others are started at the spur of the moment with no idea whatsoever what they will turn out to be until they're done. All my designs are

one-of-a-kind creations. I rarely use commercial patterns unless I want a certain tailored look. Many different materials are utilized to create my designs—all different sorts of beads and findings, feathers, boas, sequins, appliques—anything that will create that perfect effect. I'm always looking for new items to incorporate into my designs. All of these things go into a total makeover for the face, hair, outfit, and accessories resulting in an entirely new one-of-a-kind design!

I have made some wonderful friends online as a result of belonging to several fashion doll makeover groups. I owe so much to everyone who has helped me along the way. Fashion doll makeovers truly fulfill the creative part of my life.

Michelle James
2764 NW 58th Terrace
Lauderhill, FL. 33313
Email: MJames33@excite.com
Website: http://members.xoom.com/Jasmar/

Jim Howard

I am completely surprised that I am designing for dolls at this point in my life. About two years ago, an old friend of mine who is the designer of a very famous doll came to town for a signing at a doll shop near me. Just for the fun of it, I went and bought a doll and surprised the designer. The real surprise was that the doll I bought was to be one of many more to come. I was hooked! Somewhere along the way, a dear friend at the shop suggested that since I did costumes for theatre, I should try something for the doll that I was so avidly collecting. That was the beginning.

I was born in Texas many moons ago and knew from the age of four that I wanted to be an artist. When Art classes became available to me, I began a long and rewarding trip to becoming an artist. Another surprise in the long list of surprises in my life came when I accidentally became a fashion illustrator in order to finance my college education at the University of Texas. That led to a job as an illustrator at the famed Neiman Marcus store, which led to a career as a freelance illustrator in New York. Needless to say, somewhere along the way, I realized that I loved what I was doing and loved the world of fashion. I had a nice long run illustrating the work of such clients as B. Altman, Bonwit Teller, Saks Fifth Avenue, Bloomingdales, Marshall Fields, Maison Blanche, Bullock's, Garfinkles, Cosmetic Firms and Advertising Agencies.

I moved to New Mexico some years ago in semi-retirement. I now find myself, at long last, doing my own designing for dolls. The best reward is being able to please myself and not store buyers or art directors. I don't do much re-painting because my focus is the fashion, hairstyle, and accessories. I enjoy many fashion dolls. I am also making dolls in porcelain and doing a bit of sculpting in clay and oven fired clays. So, you see I'm a true "doll-o-holic!" The greatest challenge for me in creating a costume is achieving realistic scale and pleasing color effects.

Jim Howard
SOOOCHIC COUTURE
4305 Chinlee Ave. NE
Albuquerque, NM 87110
Email: sooochic@aol.com
Website: sooochic.com

Loanne Hizo Tabloach

Ulani and Noelani

My name is Loanne Hizo Tabloach of Tabloach Productions. I have been making fashion doll makeovers since June of 1999. I worked mainly with the BARBIE® doll and her friends in the past, but now am finding an interest in the Kelly® doll as well as the taller Gene® dolls and Tyler® dolls. I have a passion for creating fantasy dolls.

I started fashion doll makeovers when I was inspired by some of the artists in Jim Faraone's first book. When I started seeing the creations on eBay and that people were actually buying them, I was even more motivated. I now sell exclusively online on eBay under the id: tabloach@yahoo.com.

I've met many talented artists over the internet, and their encouragement, various styles, and different techniques have increased my desire to create every chance I get. I am a stay-at-home mom to a beautiful, healthy four- year old little girl. I have been married to the most patient and supportive man for six years. I get all my energy and creativity from them. Without the various artists and the support from my family, I wouldn't be what I most wanted to achieve today, and that is having my work published and displayed for all to see. I am very honored by this great experience.

Queen Jester - The Regal Bride

Aurum Goddess

Loanne Hizo Ostlie
Tabloach Productions
38704 Laurie Lane
Palmdale, CA. 93551
Email: Tabloach@Yahoo.com or
Loanne@Tabloach.com
Website: http://www.Tabloach.com

Rebecca Satterberg

Ascot, third place winner 1998 Gene® doll convention

My name is Rebecca Satterberg. I am a native Californian and I work as a hairstylist and group fitness instructor. I am also working towards getting a digital media certificate and am very involved in the wonderful world of doll collecting. I have always been artistic and have possessed an urge to create through crafting, sewing, and photography. Babysitting earnings helped purchase a Singer™ sewing machine when I was 12, and I have sewn everything from quilts to suits on it. Now, my favorite things to make are costumes for my seven-year old daughter Jocelyn as well as elaborate designs for fashion dolls.

I discovered the Gene® doll in 1997 and loved the "de-box and play" concept. In 1998, I started going to the Gene® doll Conventions and entering the Gene® doll Design Competitions. My *Secret Rendezvous* took 1st place in the Movie Day Wear category at the 2000 Gene® doll Convention. This has been a door to new friendships and travel, two of the most rewarding aspects of my doll passion.

One method I use to pick a competition entry is to choose a movie star icon and heavily research their movies and costumes. I then pick an outfit that really inspires me to sew and create. Next comes more research. I get every picture I can of the outfit and search for fabrics and trims that I need to recreate it in doll scale. Special attention is given to fabric, hairstyle, jewelry, and accessories. I do use patterns, but I usually tweak them into something entirely different than what they were meant to be. I then work at the outfit until it becomes what I envisioned. I usually have Ken Bartram repaint the

Blue Moon

Lucy, first place winner 1999 Gene® doll convention

doll to the likeness of the subject. Recently, my collection has branched out to the Tyler® doll, the Kitty® doll, and the Alex® doll. It's been a treat sewing for all the varied sizes and shapes.

When I get a new doll, it's almost impossible to resist taking the hair down for a restyle. I have found that boiling water works well for the Gene® doll and the Tyler® doll. I like to use small sponge rollers, chenille stems, straws, toothpicks, and permanent wave rollers as hair setting tools. A little hairstyling gel and permanent wave end-papers do wonders in getting the hair ends smoothly wrapped under. Rat tail combs and the BARBIE® doll brushes work well to complete the style.

For those of you who are interested in doing fashion doll makeovers, trust in your creativity and go for it. It can be a truly rewarding experience and very fun! A special thanks to Jim Faraone for including me in his book, to my husband, Larry, for his enthusiasm and support, and to my doll friends Debbie Silva, Kristan Molchin, Christine Quick, Kim Bennett, and Pilar Medina for their advice and encouragement.

Rebecca Satterberg
Lareba Fashion Dolls
15855 Blossom Hill Rd.
Los Gatos, CA. 95032
Email: reba@lareba.com
Website: lareba.com

Joe Tai

My name is Joe Tai, and I am a 28-year old Taiwanese boy who lives in Taiwan, and loves this Formosa island very much. I have been very interested in the beauty of art and classic music since I was a small child. I also like to design my own kind of doll. I started to design my own dolls no later than the 7th day of starting to collect BARBIE® dolls. Now, I have my own brand, box with my logo, and even my original-design shoes. I do enjoy my design career very much, and of course, fulfilling my dream by designing my own creations. Yes, I am very satisfied with myself now.

Joe Tai
3th Floor, No 14
Lane 16, Sec 2
Chung Shan Nth. Rd.
Tai Pei, Taiwan (104)
Email: whet@ms33.hinet.net
Website:
http://www.taconet.com.tw/midge/joe.htm

Christina "Bogie" Bougas

Marzipan

Wow! What an amazing joy it is to use a doll as a canvas for your own expression, and see the unpredictable creations others come up with. It's like listening to classical music. As soon as you think you've figured out the melody, the composer takes you in a totally different direction. That's when art tickles the soul. That's why I'm literally obsessed with creating a fashion doll others can build their own expression upon. When I first entered the make-over world a year ago, I was despondent by the constant horror stories I heard of manufacturers getting ticked about their dolls being altered. I can't think of anything more flattering than for a collector to love a doll so much that they want to put a piece of themselves in it. Today, almost all my free time is focused on sculpting my own 16in (41cm) fashion doll *Clea Bella* and designing clothes for her. Not only do I look forward to being a doll artist on a full-time basis, but I can't wait to see what other artists will do with my doll as well.

I start out with dozens of rough sketches and swatches of fabrics (which are far more extensive than my doll collection). I obsessively work out every detail in advance. Then I draw and paint a finished illustration that I follow as if

Princess Karrie

it were an architectural blue print. As a professional graphic designer for the film industry, I'm used to creating comps before I even begin to think about assembling a finished piece. I'm extremely jealous of people who can just pick up fabric and start creating. How fun it must be to be so free.

Yet, I know I'm blessed beyond description with all the artistic skills I have acquired over the years—sculpting, illustration, writing, acting, skating, theatre directing, stage design, costume design, graphic arts—the list is endless. Who would have thought that a shy little girl from the San Francisco Bay Area would discover so many wonderful things in less than half a lifetime? It's my sincere dream that I can continue to create art that will tickle the souls of others as much as others have tickled mine. God bless all who have the courage to express themselves!

Christina "Bogie" Bougas
411 Magnolia St., #5
South Pasadena, CA. 91030
Email: bogie3@earthlink.net

Valerie A. Hays

I'm Valerie A. Hays and I've been informed that I need to write a biography. Yikes! Well, first the basics. I was born in Japan and spent several formative years living both there and in Hawaii. Soon after my arrival to the Mainland, I discovered two things. One, Batman speaks English, not Japanese. And two, you could change the BARBIE® doll's earrings by sticking glass-headed pins through her head. I made more than my share of badly sewn BARBIE® doll clothes. After a while, I put away my BARBIE® dolls. Actually, I think most of them are buried in a back yard somewhere in Virginia.

Years passed, and I didn't think anymore about them. I went the art route, mostly pen and ink and some pastel portraits. Then my mother became a dollmaker. Correction, she became Mrs. Frankenstein. I soon became accustomed to body parts hanging in the shower to dry and bags of eyeballs on the end tables. At about the same time, I discovered Costume Design—the usual Drama Club thing. I was blinded by visions of all those wonderful movies I watched while I was growing up. A year at Boston University taught me a third thing—actors REALLY hate it when you stand them on their heads to dress them. After finding out that I wouldn't be able to design whatever I wanted whenever I wanted, Boston University and I parted ways. But I couldn't get designing out of my head. Then came Paper Dolls. This was better, but something was still missing. My mother soon sucked me into the world of porcelain doll-making. Closer, yet not quite there. It taught me to paint on a three-dimensional surface, but the bodies of the French fashion dolls were a little odd.

Then it happened. I saw my first Gene® doll, *Midnight Romance*, and I immediately began salivating and embraced the concept of "stuff lust". Little voices in my ear whispered, "Wouldn't she look fabulous dressed like Marian in *The Adventures of Robin Hood* or Paulette Goddard in *The Women*?" Soon, I was repainting them to match their rolls. Then fabrics began calling out to me, "Look! I'm shiny!" and "Go ahead, it's just a half a yard!" That half a yard deal has gotten me into so much

Art Deco Goddess

trouble. The fabrics now have their own room along with the lace and beads and a myriad of other goodies that demanded that I bring them home.

What next? I joined the Nellie Perkins chapter of the UFDC. National Conventions and competitions? Oh my! I entered my first competition in 1999 in Washington, DC. The category was "Modern doll dresses by exhibitor - circa 1950's". My piece was a changeable blue/black taffeta strapless gown with a heavily beaded bodice entitled *Northern Lights*. When she won a blue ribbon, I did the "Dance of Joy" right in the lobby of the hotel. I won my second ribbon, a red one, in 2000 with *Belle Époque*, a 1904 evening gown inspired by Worth. Jim Faraone saw *Belle* at the UFDC convention in Chicago and asked if I would like to be in this book. Again, I did the "Dance of Joy" in the hallway, scaring several distinguished ladies witless. I did the "Dance of Joy" once more when my *Belle* won a blue ribbon, Judge's Choice ribbon, and Best of Show in the amateur division at the 2000 Gene® doll convention. Does everyone have a "Dance of Joy?"

As for ideas, they come from everywhere— movies, of course, fabrics, books! I can spend days poring over books on Hollywood Costume and Fashion History! I've doodled on napkins, books, and on the occasional friend. I try to carry sketchbooks with me most of the time. After two years, I feel like I'm just starting out. The next few years should be really interesting! One quick tip: I have to admit that I cheat when I need black eyeliner for a doll. After all the color is laid down for the eyes and eyeshadow, I use a "Micron" archival ink pen with a 005 tip to lay down a thin line for eyeliner. If you lay this down over the eye paint, it won't stain the vinyl and is easy to remove. If you get some on the vinyl, remove it immediately with non-acetone solvent. One more thing, don't be obsessed when something strays from your original design and takes off in a completely different direction. My *Follies* began as an elegant 1920's evening gown with one magnificent embroidered sleeve. After taking several left turns, it became a Follies showgirl with a jeweled bosom. The main thing is to have fun with it! Otherwise, it's just work. But then again, this is coming from a woman voted "Most Likely to be Abducted by Aliens" so take it with a grain of salt.

Maeve Queen of Connacht

Valerie A. Hays
RR 1, Box 122
Lyndeboro, NH 03082
Email: shequeen@tellink.net

Lynn Smith

I was born in Sarnia Ontario Canada, the year that the BARBIE® doll debuted. Like most little girls, I grew up playing with BARBIE® dolls. I loved my dolls more than any other toy. Compared to most of my friends, I had a rather large and varied collection. I never missed an opportunity to go shopping with my mother and grandmother on Saturday mornings to the local Farmer's Market for hand-made doll clothes. A local woman had a stall in the back corner of the Market, and her tables were covered with the most beautiful doll clothes. I think those hand-made doll clothes were the inspiration I needed to learn to knit and sew for my own dolls. Neither my mother nor my grandmother sewed, so I was forced to figure it out for myself. My childhood attempts weren't wonderful, but I continued to knit and sew long after my dolls were stored away. My other lifelong interest was drawing. In high school, I took every art course and technical art course offered. I also took a few courses in college. No matter the medium, portraits were my favorite subjects.

I spent most of my adult life living in Toronto, working in a variety of jobs, none of them artistic. In the fall of 1998, I was taking night school courses at a local college. I was unhappy with my job, so I was studying to

teach introductory computer adult-education courses. The Teaching Adult Education course that I was taking required me to teach a 20-minute class to my fellow students on any subject that I chose. I figured it might be a bit too difficult to teach a computer class in a room with no computer, so I chose to teach a class on how to make upholstered doll furniture—something I was working on for my two young nieces. The class was well received. I got a lot of encouragement from friends and family to sell my furniture and to offer classes on the subject. I decided to do just that. Around the same time, I pulled my childhood dolls out of their 30-year home in my parent's attic. After almost 30 years, I was back playing with my dolls.

While doing my doll furniture, I also started building my own website, LDSmith Designs for Dolls. While searching the internet for doll-related sites, I discovered email groups at Onelist. I joined a few of these groups, and through those groups, I discovered fashion doll makeovers. I was fascinated by what I saw, and knew I would love it before I had even started working on my first doll. I ordered Jim's first two fashion doll makeover books and started working on my first doll around Christmas of 1998. Shortly after I finished my first doll, Jim's books arrived in the mail. Between Jim's books and my online friends, I received a great deal of information about doing fashion

Sherry and Glenda

doll makeovers. I did lots of experimenting and was soon developing my own techniques.

When I first started fashion doll makeovers, there weren't many makeover tips posted on the web. Other people new to the hobby were asking the same questions that I had asked, so I decided to add some of my own tips to my website. Thus, I began building my Fashion Doll Customizing Tips pages. With contributions from many fellow makeover artists, it quickly grew to be the largest collection of makeover tips on the web. Writing for my website gave me the confidence to submit my how-to project ideas to *Miller's®* fashion doll magazine. My article "Microbraid Hair Replacement" appeared in the "Project" section of the October 1999 issue. Unfortunately, *Miller's®* was sold and other articles that I wrote have yet to be printed.

In October 1999, my husband and I sold our house in Toronto and moved temporarily to my hometown of Sarnia. We stayed there for a few months until my husband got a job in a small community near Windsor Ontario. Presently, we live on a farm in that area. The Detroit area has the closest doll clubs to my home, and in January 2000, I went to my first meeting of the Fashion Doll Collector's Club Great Lakes Region. I haven't missed a meeting since. I am the Chairperson of the Workshop Committee for the 2001 National Barbie® Doll Convention, the webmaster of the convention website, and editor and publisher of the club's monthly newsletter.

I work with a variety of fashion dolls and I'm always looking for new and different dolls to work on. I love experimenting with new techniques and materials. I draw inspiration from movies and TV shows, as well as from new materials I find around the house or while shopping. When I first started doing makeovers, I found it difficult to describe my style because each of my dolls looked so different. One thing that has been said repeatedly about my dolls is that they look

**Warrior Prince and
Rasta Steve**

very realistic. These comments led me to do portrait dolls such as the Gene® doll as Marilyn Monroe, Generation Girl® Tori as Gwyneth Paltrow, and the Gene® doll as Queen Amidala. Details such as individual teeth in my open-mouth dolls, resculpted features, or handmade footwear are some of the trademarks of my work. When I'm not doing a portrait doll or commissioned work, I let the doll evolve on its own. It rarely turns out like expect, which I find very exciting.

It has been difficult to find time to work on my dolls or write as much as I would like during this past year. I have too many ideas and never enough time, but I plan to continue my doll makeovers and my writing in addition to developing many new doll-related projects as time permits. Attending the 2000 National Barbie® Doll Convention in Tulsa and being a member of the Great Lakes Club has given me the opportunity to meet many wonderful and talented people that I had previously known only online or read about in Jim's first three fashion doll makeover books. I'm looking forward to the 2001 Convention in Dearborn. Plus, I can't wait to see what Jim plans to include in this, his newest book *4th Fashion Doll Makeovers*.

Lynn Smith
LDSmith Designs for Dolls
P.O. Box 1356
Royal Oak, MI. 48068-1356
Email: ldsmith@email.com
Website: www.designsfordolls.com

Freddy Tan

Millennium Crystals Goddess

My name is Freddy Tan. I'm from the tiny, but beautiful country of Singapore. I was not really into dolls when I was young. I liked action figure toys. When I got tired of buying off the shelves, I started to create my own toys. I used a lot of mixed media in my works. I always liked the female action figures and things dealing with fantasy. One day, I thought that the BARBIE® doll could be an excellent choice to customize and here I am. I've created lots of different characters with the BARBIE® doll and some other fashion dolls.

I like fantasy-type dolls now and Haute Couture fashions inspire me a great deal. As you can see, most of my dolls are inspired by fantasy, yet they are glamorous. I always like my dolls to look like pieces of art rather than just a pretty doll, which is probably due to my Fine Arts background. I use the finest materials and real crystals on them. I want them to look precious and very eye-catching. My designs are mostly inspired by fantasy books. My favorite artists are Boris Vallejo and Jullie Bell. Also, the fantasy doll artist, Renee Coughlan, often inspires me.

I try my very best not to imitate other artists or designer's styles. I'm always looking for new fabrics, new media, and colors for facial painting. I love to create my dolls with different looks. I'm very fortunate to have a family that is so supportive, and I am grateful for the many collectors that value my skills and talent. Without them, I don't think I'd be here today. Thank you very much and God bless.

Freddy Tan
501 Orchard Rd. #02-06
Wheelock Place, Singapore 238880
(65) 733 7377
Email: dollzinc@singnet.com.sg

Millennium Haute Couture

John Patrick Zaragoza

I am a Los Angeles based designer and I share my home with one roommate, three dogs, and over 1,500 dolls. An art major in college, I have worked in advertising most of my life. I fell into design quite by accident. Christmas 1995 became a turning point when a present in the form of a Marilyn Monroe doll changed my whole life. The doll remained on my mantel until I began stretching fabric swatches around her. As time passed, I began experimenting with the hair, which became my favorite step. Suddenly, the doll world was opened to me.

Recalling my sister's titian Midge® doll dressed in *Modern Art* reminded me how dolls, and anything miniature for that matter, fascinated me. Those tiny shoes! Always a very hands on person, I spent much of my childhood constructing everything from toys to tree houses. My taste in dolls has now dwindled it's way down to an eclectic, integrated collection of both female, male, vintage, and sexy fashion dolls, but I never limit myself to any one product. Since my designs tend towards the exotic, I find ethnic dolls the most fun to use. Rescued dolls are the most rewarding to work with. Unless it's fantasy, striving for realism is my goal.

Both self and book taught, all work is done by hand including eyelashes, individual braids, and of course, one sequin or bead sewn on at a time. Special dolls are subject to availability, but basic styles can be transferred or mixed on various dolls or customer-provided dolls. I thank God constantly for being able to do something that I really love.

John Patrick Zaragoza
636½ N. Orange Dr.
Los Angeles, CA. 90036
Email: zaragozajpatrick@aol.com

Tom Courtney

Photo by Brian Shumaker, Shumaker Photography, Vancouver, WA.

I have always enjoyed creating miniatures. My brothers and sister also share a creative eye toward miniature, whether it is a model airplane painted to exacting detail or the classical world of creative photography. I learned basic sewing from my mother and I took one clothing construction class while studying fashion merchandising and marketing in school. Building on these skills took a great deal of time and mistakes. For example, I hesitated looking at expensive fabrics for many years. Better quality fabrics sew differently than lesser quality fabrics. I learned through practice that it was necessary from time to time to "play" with the more expensive fabrics in order to understand their drape and tailoring qualities. Yes, I ruined many gorgeous textiles, but the knowledge I gained from this was well worth it. I guess that's one reason I turned from human-scale to dolls.

My mother collected dolls since she was a child. She and my father built a small collection for my sister who lost interest in these dolls because she could only look at them. To think of giving a child a doll that he or she could not play with—how criminal! But, Janet did have her play fashion dolls of never-ending variety. I loved Janet's fashion dolls of the 60's and 70's. Nevertheless, I was always drawn to the dolls that "shouldn't be played with". In our later years, a fire swept through the house and brought a fair amount of smoke damage to these ladies. My mother and I took them in and I watched Mama care and clean each one. That was what really cinched it for me. Some 17 years later, I am now the proud owner of a very extensive and diverse collection of modern fashion dolls—and I play with each and every one! Which one is my favorite?

There are a few: A Scarlett O'Hara and Rhett Butler made from cloth by the loving hands of my mother; my redressed Kitty Collier® Bride doll; my "Betsy Globrightly" redressed Betsy McCall® doll by Nancy Schroeder; a Sherry Miller repainted Tyler Wentworth® doll to look like my niece, Elizabeth; a rooted blond Cissy®; a re-dressed "Gothic Kid" BARBIE® doll by my friends, Dana and Eddie; and a pair of Gene® dolls that I redressed as "Patsy and Edina" from the British Sitcom, "Absolutely Fabulous".

Since then, I continued to dabble with human-scale clothing; but I migrated into using quality fabrics for dolls because they deserve it (not to mention it was cheaper and construction took less time). Today, I am always learning from other artists and masters that share their ideas of dreams and creativity. You never stop learning, and to think you know it all is doing yourself a great disservice. If I can ask Robert Tonner about a seamline or Mel Odem about the use of color or if I can ask any of my doll-collecting friends for their opinions, then I can learn and therefore teach others. This becomes a never-ending cycle of taking and giving knowledge.

Anyone can sew clothing. The design composition is what makes it pleasing to the eye. When I first gained interest in fashion and historical costume, the one thing that eluded me was the importance of the design composition. Now, I drew for years, and for a headstrong youth focused on a life in fashion, I felt it was important to convey my individuality as an artist. Well, that probably explains why I ended up pursuing a career with the Federal Government and subsequently, software design. Around 1992-93, I finally realized I needed some much-needed instruction in areas of which I knew very little. That's when I enrolled in a couple of classes at a local junior college. The bottom line is, if you are one of those folks that dreams of being able to draw and can admit to yourself that you do need instruction in

design composition, there are two wonderful books that turned my work into art. *Drawing on the Right Side of the Brain* and *Drawing on the Artist Within* are both books by Betty Edwards (visit her website at http://www.drawright.com). These books brought a profound understanding of how we see things and how to capture it in artistic composition in the same ways that we learned to "draw" letters in handwriting. Creativity needs exercising just as muscles do. These two books taught my artist within to "work-out" regularly. Your results will astonish you. Imagine, create, and dream...that's my creed. Understand that learning is light, and remember to always glow brightly.

Tom Courtney
1521 North Colonial Ct.
Arlington, VA. 22209
Email: memnochva@hotmail.com
Website: http://www.alwaysglowbrightly.com

How To Enhance Your Own Fashion Doll Wonder

Photos by Kerry Anne Faraone

I have featured many artists in this book who create unusual and fantasy-type dolls. I thought it would be fun to teach you some unusual techniques to enhance your dolls. Being creative is the most enjoyable part of fashion doll makeovers. Experimenting and coming up with something new that no one else has done is one of the tricks to success.

I have also received numerous emails and letters from readers asking for instructions on how I elaborated on the molded hair dolls (which I teach in book 3) using beads and buckram. With no secrets here, I am more than happy to share the techniques with you. If there is anything you would like to see in my "How To" sections, don't be shy. Just email or write with your suggestions. My series of books are for YOU, so don't hesitate to make suggestions.

Enhancing Your Molded Hair Creations

Beaded Hairstyles

Tools needed: Long needle, thread, and small, medium and large beads.

Start by knotting a tiny bead on the end of your double-threaded needle. Insert it into the neck opening and out of the top of the head **(Step 1)** (You can come out the top of the head for a "bun" effect or out towards the forehead for a "Betty Grable" look. You can even come out towards the nape of the neck for a "Flamenco" look). String your largest bead (I usually use pearls or clear plastic beads) onto the thread. Insert the needle back into the head and out the neck opening to sew the center bead in place. **(Step 2)**

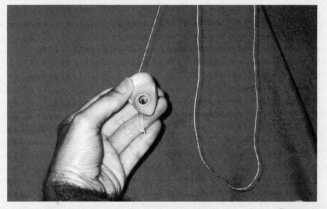

Step 1

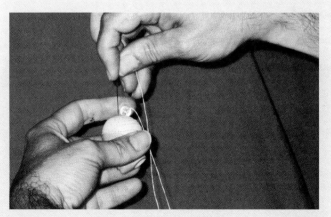

Step 2

Beaded Hairstyles

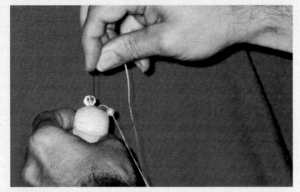

Step 3

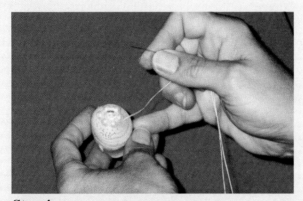

Step 4

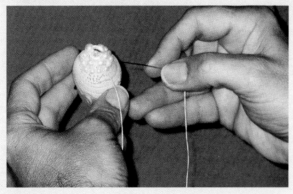

Step 5

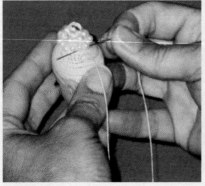

Step 6

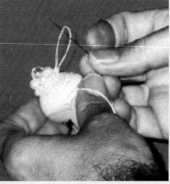

Step 7

Step 8

Again, insert the needle through the neck opening and out the top of the head. This time, string your medium-sized bead onto the thread and insert it back into the head. **(Step 3)** Sew a circle of the medium-sized beads around the large bead in the center using the same technique. So that you don't come out the same hole and pull your thread out, come up through the head a little in front of the last bead. **(Step 4)** Now, take your smallest-sized beads and sew them in a circle around the medium-sized beads. **(Step 5)** When you have completed the ring of small beads, catch the thread under the beads and slide your needle through. **(Step 6)** Then knot your thread. **(Step 7)** I suggest knotting the thread in about 4 places to firmly hold your beads to the head. Then begin to apply the modeling paste to the doll's hair using the steps for molded hair given in book 3. Here is one of the unique styles that you can create for your doll's hair. **(Step 8)**

Extra tips: You can have fun using all types of beads. Start a row of medium-sized beads going from the forehead straight down the back of the head to the nape of the neck. Then outline the row of medium-sized beads with the small beads. This makes a great French braid effect. Or just sew one circle of small beads around the crown of the head to make a German-type braided look. The ideas are endless.

Tools needed: Long needle, thread, scissors, and buckram.

Take a strip of buckram approximately 5/8in x 8in (2cm x 20cm) and roll it twice around your pinky. **(Step 9)** Sew your loop together to hold it in place. **(Step 10)** Curl the opposite end and sew it in place forming 2 loops. **(Step 11)** Once you have the loops sewn securely, sew them into the head just as you did for the beaded hairstyles. **(Step 12)** Remember, use the tiny bead on your double-threaded needle to anchor your thread on the inside of the doll's head so that the thread does not slip through. Once you have the curls sewn onto the head, follow the instructions in book 3 to apply the modeling paste. **Caution:** When applying your first thin coat of modeling paste, use a VERY thin coat on the buckram curls. If you put a thick coat on them right away, the buckram will soften causing your curls to collapse. By putting a VERY thin coat of the modeling paste onto the curls (even just on the top or inner area of the curls) and letting it dry overnight, the buckram curls will stiffen enough to put on a thicker coat for the second application. The fun part is seeing how many unusual hairstyles you can come up with **(Step 13)**

Extra tips: Again, have fun with this and see what other creations you come up with using the buckram. You can create as many curls as you'd like, or make thicker or thinner curls. Imagination is the root of all things.

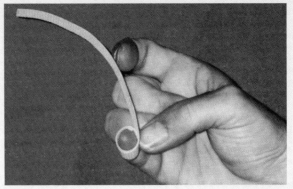

Step 9

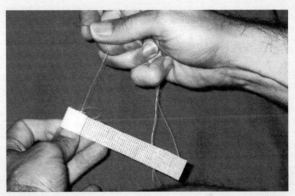

Step 10

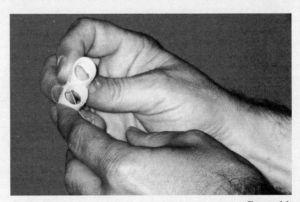

Step 11

Step 13

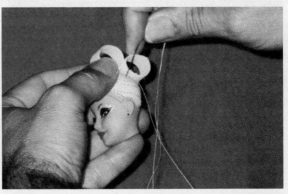

Step 12

The Mohawk

Tools needed: Buckram, long needle, thread, marking pen, and scissors.

Place the side of your doll's head on a piece of buckram and trace around it. **(Step 14)** This outline of the doll's head allows you to draw your Mohawk design. **(Step 15)** Extend the bottom line of the Mohawk so that you have enough buckram to attach to your doll's head. **(Step 16)** Cut the section that will be sewn to your doll's head in 4 places. **(Step 17)** Bend each flap in an opposite direction. **(Step 18)** Using the same techniques as the previous styles, sew these flaps onto your doll's head and knot it securely to the head. **(Step 19)** Now you're ready to use the modeling paste. Remember to use a VERY light first coat of modeling paste on the Mohawk and let it dry overnight. Now you can create your own funky dolls for those nights on the town. **(Step 20)**

Extra tips: I am still experiment with the molded hair dolls. In future experiments I plan to use pipe cleaners or wire as curls and then use the modeling paste over them. See what unique things you can come up with on your own molded hair dolls.

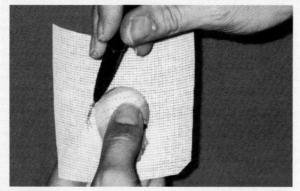

Step 14

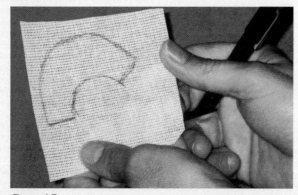

Step 15

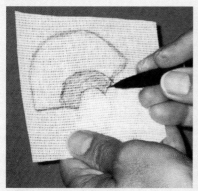

Step 16

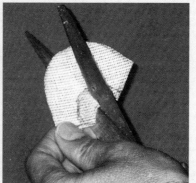

Step 17

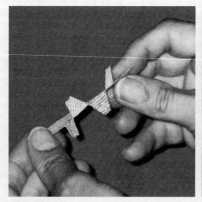

Step 18

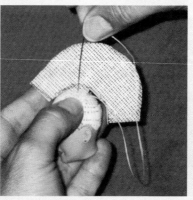

Step 19

Step 20

Tools needed: Needle, thread, seam binding, pins, needle-nose pliers, and fabric.

To begin with, take a strip of ½in (1cm) seam binding and cut a length that will encircle the doll's head. **(Step 21)** Take 4 straight pins, and with your needle-nose pliers, cut them a little short and on an angle so that they still have pointed tips. **(Step 22)** Place the seam binding around the doll's head. Hold the seam binding in place by putting a pin in the front of the doll's head to. **(Step 23)** Also, place the pins in each side of the head to hold the seam binding in place. **(Step 24)** Where the ends of the seam binding meet, fold one end over the other and sew the two sides together. Place your final pin into the seam binding at the back of the head. (You can also do this with the head removed from your doll. Using an anchor bead, go through the neck hole, baste the seam binding right to the doll's head for extra support, and then remove the pins). **(Step 25)** Use the same color seam binding and thread. I'm only using contrasting colors so you can see each step. The color of the seam binding should match your fabric and beaded design. Then cut a circle of fabric that will cover your doll's head. **(Step 26)** Sew it onto the seam binding around the doll's head. **(Step 27)** Once you have sewn the fabric around the doll's head, take nips and tucks to the fabric to smooth it over the doll's head. **(Step 28)** Don't worry about your doll looking like Frankenstein or a casualty victim because your beadwork will cover all the hidden secrets. You now have your "canvas" for creating wonder beadwork hairstyles.

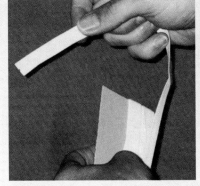
Step 21

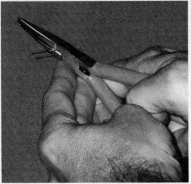
Step 22

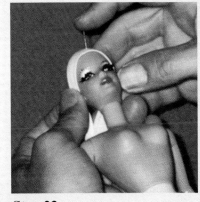
Step 23

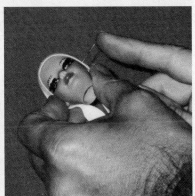
Step 24

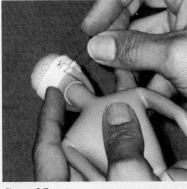
Step 25

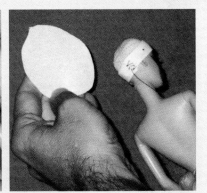
Step 26

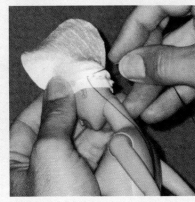
Step 27

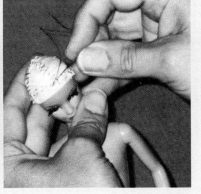
Step 28

Beaded Loop Hair

Tools needed: Needle, thread, sequins, and seed beads.

Start at the edge of the fabric-covered head and sew each sequin by placing it facetted side up. Then string 5 seed beads (or number of beads you decide) onto your thread. **(Step 29)** Go back through the hole of the same sequin and into the fabric canvas. Come out where you will place your next sequin. **(Step 30)** Repeat this process making loops around your doll's head until you reach the top where you'll knot it off. Voila! You have a fascinating new look. **(Step 31)**

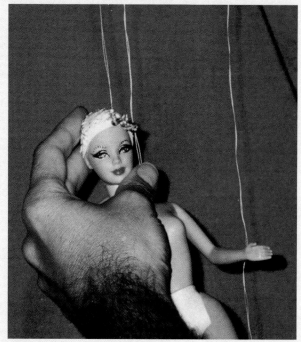

Step 29

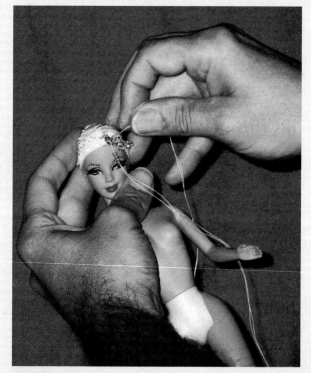

Step 30

Step 31

Tools needed: Needle, thread, needle-nose pliers, seed beads, and flowers.

I usually buy the small clusters of ribbon roses at the craft stores or in the craft section of a store. **(Step 32)** Clip off one of the flowers. With your double-threaded needle, go through the flower and out the other end to thread it. Be sure to catch the end piece of the ribbon flower so that it doesn't unravel. **(Step 33)** You may need your needle-nose pliers to get the needle through. Sew the flower onto the doll's fabric covered head. **(Step 34)** Then thread 5 seed beads (or any desired number). **(Step 35)** Go back into the fabric creating a loop. **(Step 36)** Continue sewing interchanging flowers and loops of beads around the head till you end at the top of the doll's head. **(Step 37)** Once finished, you have the look of a breath of Springtime. **(Step 38)**

Step 32

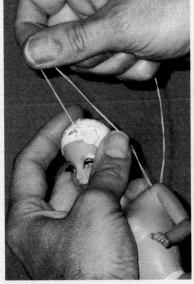

Step 33

Step 34

Step 38

Step 35

Step 36

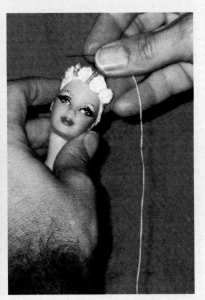

Step 37

Breaded Strands of Hair or Fringe

Tools needed: Needle, thread, sequins, and beads.

Many people have asked me how to do beaded fringe on outfits. Well, the same technique works for using strands of beads for the hair or the clothes. First, straight stitch sequins (as explained in book 2) onto the entire fabric canvas that's on your doll's head assuming you are making hair. I am showing only one row here. If you are making fringe for clothing, you can skip this step. **(Step 39)** Then thread your needle so that you are only using one strand. Thread a tiny seed bead (or any end bead you'd like to use) onto your thread. **(Step 40)** Take the free end of your thread and re-thread it back into the needle's eye so that there are two ends going through the eye. **(Step 41)** Now, you have a tiny anchor-bead at the end of your double thread, which will support the other beads that you string. **(Step 42)** String your design of beads the desired length for your doll's hair or clothing. **(Step 43)** Then take your needle and strand of beads and beginning at the edge of the fabric cap, sew the strand into the hole of one of the sequins. Pull it tight. **(Step 44)** Tightly knot it several times underneath another sequin so your knots do not show. Once it is knotted tightly, give the strand a gentle tug to loosen it a tiny bit giving your strand, or fringe a nice swing. **(Step 45)** Once you are comfortable with all of these techniques, you can combine them to create a truly distinct look. **(Step 46)**

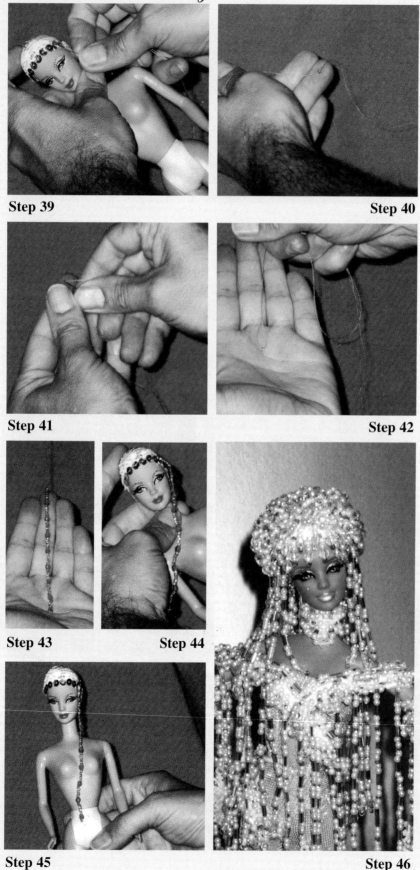

Step 39

Step 40

Step 41

Step 42

Step 43

Step 44

Step 45

Step 46

Tools needed: Needle, thread, beads, and flowers.

As with the strands or fringe, create an anchor bead on your thread. **(Step 47)** Thread the desired number of seed beads onto your thread and top them off with a slightly larger bead. **(Step 48)** This larger bead will hold your flowers in place. The best flowers to use are lilies-of-the-valley or any flowers with that shape and size. Pop off one of the flowers. Be sure not to lose the plastic center of each flower. **(Step 49)** First, thread the little plastic center onto your thread **(Step 50)** Slide down so that it hooks onto the last large bead that you threaded. **(Step 51)** Now, slide the flower on so that it catches on the small plastic center and stays in place. **(Step 52)** Continue with your 5 seed beads or whatever length you choose. Remember to add that slightly larger bead before adding your flower pieces. **(Step 53)**

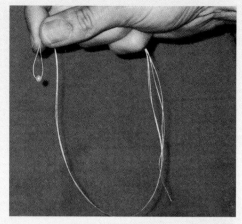

Step 47

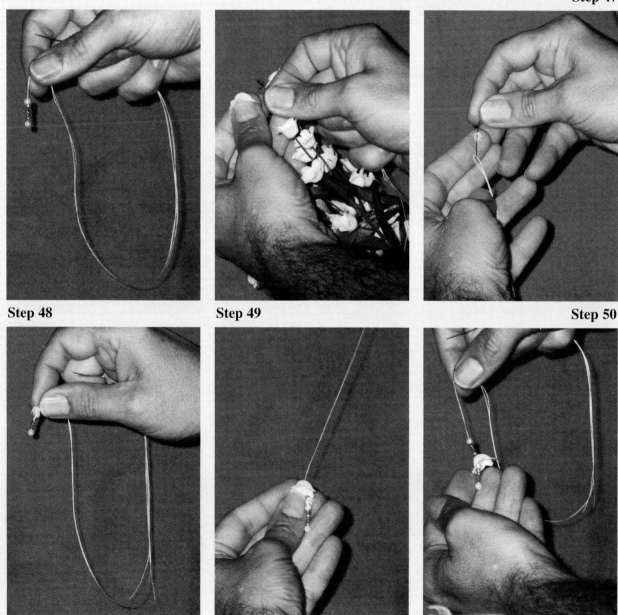

Step 48

Step 49

Step 50

Step 51

Step 52

Step 53

Cascades of Flowered Hair

Step 54

Step 55

Once you've achieved your desired length, sew it tightly into the hole of a sequin (once again, your whole fabric cap should be covered with the straight sewn sequins.) Knot it behind one of the other sequins. **(Step 54)** Once knotted, give it a slight tug to loosen the strand. **(Step 55)** This technique can add a real punch to your fairies or fantasy-type creations. **(Step 56) (Step 57)**

Step 56

Step 57

Fairy Wings

Tools needed: 2½in (4cm) wired ribbon, scissors, needle, thread, acrylic paint, pearl tipped pins, large beads, and Styrofoam®.

Step 58

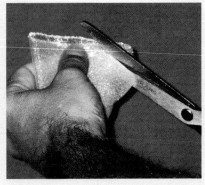

Step 59

Step 60

To make easy fairy wings, simply take a 2½in (4cm) strip of wired ribbon and cut it to the length that you want for your wings. **(Step 58)** Fold the ribbon in half and cut a curve at the end of the ribbon. **(Step 59)** When unfolded, you will see you have two even curves at each end of the ribbon. **(Step 60)** You can also fold the ribbon and cut any shape that you'd like. **(Step 61)** Remember that the tips I give in my books are your basics and I always encourage you to take everything a step further. Once you have your shape cut out, put a pearl tipped pin through the ribbon and add a large bead onto the pin **(Step 62)** Then, pin your wings to a piece of Styrofoam®. **(Step 63)** The large bead will raise your wings off the base so that the paint will not stick to the surface. Next, simply choose the wing design and paint it onto the ribbon wings. **(Step 64)** Once you have painted your wings, you may want to highlight them with other colors. Experiment and have fun creating your own wing designs. When the paint is thoroughly dried on your wings, remove them from the Styrofoam®. With needle and thread, begin to shirr the wings in the center. **(Step 65)** I usually shirr it half way, tack it, and then continue shirring the wings to the end sewing it together. **(Step 66)** Once sewn, you can now sew it to the back of your doll's outfit **(Step 67)** Cover your threads with a wrap of seed beads on your thread. Winged dolls can cover a vast array of ideas like my winged insect series. **(Step 68)**

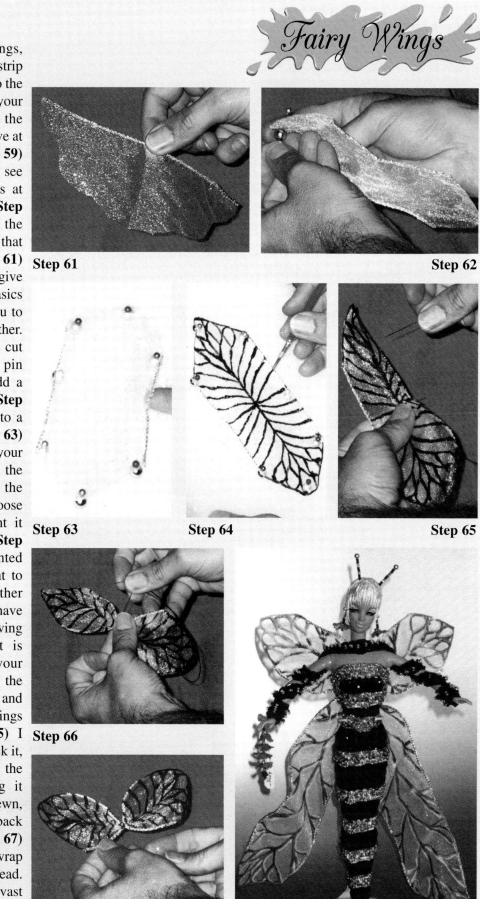

Step 61

Step 62

Step 63

Step 64

Step 65

Step 66

Step 67

Step 68

Fabric Wings and Appliques

Tools needed: Needle, thread, graph paper, scissors, buckram, marking pen, fabric, paint brush, paint, ¾in (2cm) hem lace, beads, and sequins.

Fold a piece of graph paper in half and draw one side of the wings or applique that you would like. **(Step 69)** Cut out your design and unfold the graph paper. This gives you an image that is the same on both sides. **(Step 70)** This technique works well when creating patterns so that both sides of the pattern match. Trace your design onto a piece of buckram and cut it out. **(Step 71)** Then baste a nice satin or satin-finish fabric to your buckram piece. **(Step 72)** Cut the excess fabric from around the buckram, flip it over, and baste another piece of fabric to the other side. **(Step 73)** Cut the excess fabric from this side as well. **(Step 74)** Paint the white edges that show with paint that matches your fabric. **(Step 75)** (If you'd like to use a seam binding or ribbon to edge your applique, then you can skip Step 75). Use hem lace. **(Step 76)**

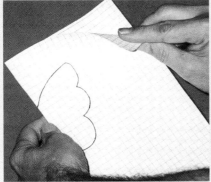

Step 69

Step 70

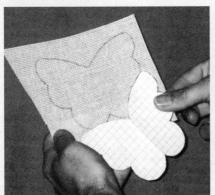

Step 71

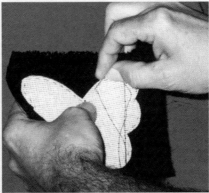

Step 72

Step 73

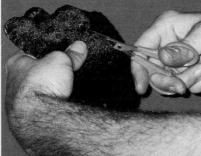

Step 74

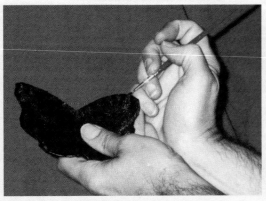

Step 75

Step 76

Fold it over the edge of your wing or applique and baste it into place. **(Step 77)** When basting on the hem lace, use very small stitches on one side. This will be your finished back in case you choose not to bead the back. You can do larger stitches on the other side. The larger stitch side will be hidden with your beads and sequins. Finish off your hem lace. **(Step 78)** On the side with the larger stitches, draw on the design and finish with beading and sequins. **(Step 79)** The back of your wings or appliques now has a beautiful finished look instead of cardboard or oak tag glued to them. **(Step 80)** Remember that the back of your creations should look as good as the front. No one enjoys buying a beautiful doll after seeing a photo of it and upon receiving it finds that the back looks like a nightmare. With imagination, you can create beautiful designs with beaded and sequined wings and appliques. **(Step 81)** **(Step 82)**

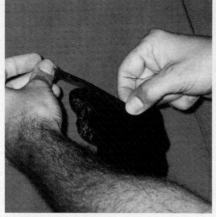

Step 77

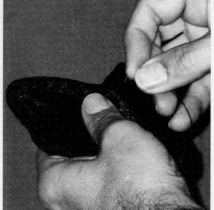

Step 78

Step 79

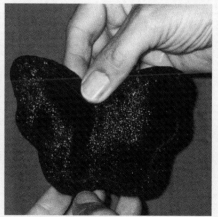

Step 80

Step 81

Step 82

Gloves

Tools needed: Thin stretch fabric, scissors, sewing machine, needle, thread, tweezers, and paintbrush. I always say that accessories really make dolls stand out.

One accessory that I usually notice are the gloves or a lack thereof, so I decided to share my personal pattern that I created for making gloves.

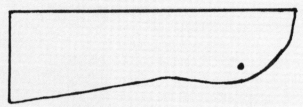

Cut out the pattern and sew the top hem on your gloves. **(Step 83)** I always set my sewing machine stitch spacing between 0 and 1. Fold your glove and tack it with a needle and thread to hold the top of the gloves even. **(Step 84)** Place the top of your glove under the foot of your sewing machine and slowly start to sew down the side of the glove to the dot. Hold the beginning stitch by first going forward, reverse, and then forward again. **(Step 85)** If you don't want to mark the dot on your glove, the dot is about the center of the rounded bottom part of the pattern. Turn the glove at a 45-degree angle and sew only 2 stitches. **(Step 86)** This will form the tip of the doll's thumb. Turn the glove again and sew 7 stitches up, which will form the thumb. **(Step 87)** Angle the glove again and sew down 9 stitches, which begins to form the mitt on the glove. **(Step 88)**

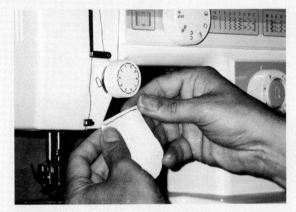

Step 83

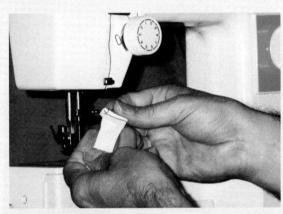

Step 84

Step 85

Step 86

Step 87

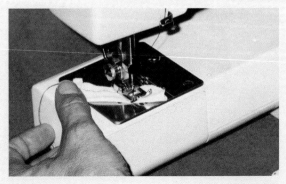

Step 88

Turn the glove once more to finish the end of the glove mitt. Secure the last stitch in the same way that you secured the first by going forward and then reversing with your machine to finish it off tightly. **(Step 89)** Now you can see the form of the glove on the fabric. You can make the gloves as long or as short as you'd like. **(Step 90)** Trim off the excess fabric. **(Step 91)** Insert tweezers into the glove. **(Step 92)** Grab hold of the inside tip of the glove with your tweezers. **(Step 93)** Holding onto the inside tip of the glove, pull your tweezers out and your glove will turn right side out with ease. **(Step 94)** Using the tip of a paintbrush, poke into the glove to straighten out the mitt and thumb sections. **(Step 95)** With a little practice, you'll be knocking out gloves with the pros.

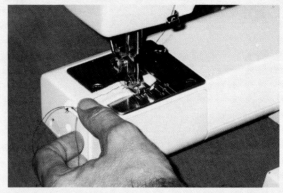

Step 89

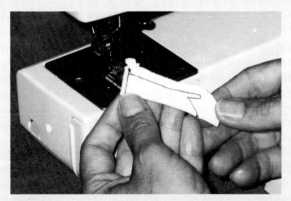

Step 90

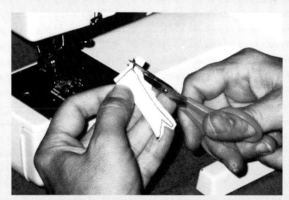

Step 91

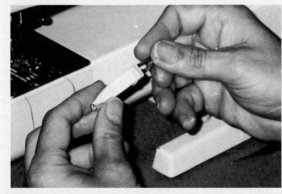

Step 92

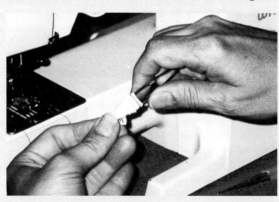

Step 93

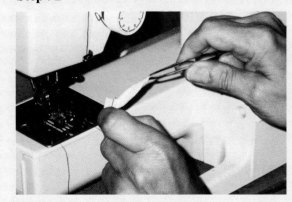

Step 94

Step 95

About the Author

The winner of two crystal trophies at the 2000 BMAA Awards from *Barbie® Bazaar*, Jim Faraone, is an avid doll collector with a collection of over 3,500 dolls of all kinds. He is not just a doll collector but also collects paper dolls, paper toys, 40's, 50's and 60's plastic dollhouse furniture, children's aluminum cookware and accessories, celebrity-autographed photos and more as time goes on.

A respected artist, Jim has had his artwork featured twice in the UFDC (United Federation of Doll Clubs) publication *Doll News*. His award winning pieces of artwork have also been featured souvenirs at many conventions and has been on display at the Metropolitan Museum of Art in New York City.

Jim's articles on the BARBIE® doll, advertising dolls, celebrity dolls, fashion doll makeovers and paper dolls have appeared numerous times in several magazines including *Miller's, Contemporary Doll Collector* and *Doll Reader*. He has also covered many of the various doll and paper doll conventions in magazines and on the internet.

Jim is internationally known in the collecting field and is actively involved with many of the conventions. He organizes and runs many of the Artist's Galleries, which feature the new work of professional and non-professional artists. Jim is an avid believer in supporting the well-deserved artists and giving those people the recognition that they deserve. Jim has been commended several times for his strong determination in giving the artists a place in the spotlight. He has run several workshops and seminars on painting techniques, paper doll artwork, getting published and the recreation of the fashion doll, taking each budding artist step-by-step through the trials and tribulations of creating.

Jim and his collectibles have appeared in several magazines and newspapers around the world, including the front cover of *USA Today*. His recreated fashion dolls have also appeared on several television news segments, as well as in magazines and newspapers. He likes variety, so he creates everything from Haute Couture ensembles, caricature dolls, vintage suits, to hand-beaded and sequined evening gowns. His newest line consists of fantasy creations and his "Insect" line, which turns the fashion doll into various types of insects, has been a big hit as everyone is now starting their own "bug" collection of Faraone Originals. His intricate beadwork has astounded many collectors who own one of his detailed creations in their collection. All of his full-skirted creations have beneath the flowing skirts, tiny lace trimmed panties, garter belt with rhinestone "clasps," and stockings. He enjoys adding the small detail work on his creations. Even a few fashion doll manufacturers have praised his work and creations.

Jim Faraone has made his hobby a lifetime infatuation and the joy; comfort and friendships he's made over the years are always treasured. He truly enjoys hearing from collectors and artists around the world. Feel free to contact him with any comments or feedback on his books or become a member of his free internet list at FashionDollMakeovers-subscribe@yahoogroups.com.

Jim Faraone
19109 Silcott Springs Rd.
Purcellville, VA. 20132
(540) 338-3621
Email: jimfaraone@erols.com
Website: http://www.erols.com/jimfaraone/